(Continued from front flap)

reasons for or against some contention. The difficulty with the first is that there is, in education, often no rational way to criticize or assess it; the difficulty with the second, that there are no rational criteria for assessing evaluative arguments that purport to answer the question "What should be taught?" The third use of argument, Mr. Bandman believes, may represent a way out of the impasse posed by the other two. An argument in the third sense may be thought of as "cogent"—one that is compelling, convincing, or telling to the mind. The meaning of a cogent argument in education is explicated and illustrated through a critical treatment and extension of the "good reasons" approach in ethics. Critical reference is also made to the Ordinary Language analysis of recent metaphysical and theological arguments.

Bertram Bandman is associate professor of Philosophy at Long Island University.

Studies in Educational Theory of the John Dewey Society **NUMBER 4**

The Place of Reason in Education

The Commission on Studies in Educational Theory
Appointed by the John Dewey Society

Frederick Ellis
Western Washington State College

Ward Madden
Brooklyn College,
The City University of New York

Israel Scheffler
Harvard University

Robert Mason, Chairman
University of Pittsburgh

The Place of Reason in Education

by BERTRAM BANDMAN

OHIO STATE UNIVERSITY PRESS

Library of Congress Catalogue Card Number: 66-25169

To Elsie

Foreword

In sponsoring the "Studies in Educational Theory," the John Dewey Society has had as its major objective to bring to the attention of thoughtful educators, hard at work in classrooms and administrative offices, and in the preparation of teachers, technical scholarly works that apply relevant philosophical tenets to current educational problems and concerns.

Readers who have not followed recent developments in formal academic philosophy will find that some parts of this book are devoted to what seem to be the purely technical and special concerns of formal philosophy, and that others belabor, elaborately and unduly, what at first appear to be quite obvious matters. The book is vulnerable to both charges inasmuch as the answer to the fundamental question, What should be taught?, is at once patently obvious and anguishingly complex. For even when we are certain of what it is exactly that we believe is right and true, we continue to face questions that relate, in a complex network of interconnections, to the problem of what, indeed, *should* be taught. It is to these disturbing questions that Professor Bandman addresses himself by applying some of the techniques of modern analytical philosophy to the study of education.

Professor Bandman's position is that what we believe about reality, knowledge, and goodness can make a good deal of difference in education, and that a carefully reasoned educational program will draw, quite properly, on both moral and metaphysical notions. He insists, however, at the same time, that pedagogical conditions must also be satisfied; for, he argues, the problem of whether a subject can be taught meaningfully—that is, so that it is genuinely learned and not merely memorized—is a consideration as important as whether the subject itself is true and valuable. And this is really a most remarkable argument to emerge from an investigation such as we have here, for it dignifies pedagogy by maintaining that its findings are necessary and crucial in educational decision-making.

Professor Bandman's investigation into the place of reason in education is in the grand tradition of philosophy as a search for measure or principle. To those who respond to the question, What should be taught?, capriciously and according to the prevailing fashion of the day, it will seem a thoroughly unnecessary and precious enterprise. For those educators who suffer in the search for a just measure by which judgment can be rendered, however, it will prove to have profound meaning. Important questions, such as What should be taught?, need to be given reasoned answers if we are to maintain a modicum of freedom; for decisions involving the public good that are based on capricious adherence to fashionable theories that are widely held rest solely upon power; and justice, in this instance, becomes merely service to the interests of the stronger.

The Commission on Studies in Educational Theory of the John Dewey Society, which recommended publication of *The Place of Reason in Education* to the Society's Executive Board, has played a considerable part in the critical evaluation of the manuscript during its final revision for publication. With the author, the members of the Commission are grateful to other consultants who evaluated the work in progress and made suggestions for its improvement. Of particular value has been the advice of Professor Arno Bellack, of Teachers College, Columbia University; Professor James McClellan, of Temple University; and Professor Joe Burnett, of the University of Illinois and president of the John Dewey Society.

ROBERT E. MASON

University of Pittsburgh
June 24, 1966

Preface

I tried to write this book in the conviction that reason has a role to play in human affairs and that the way of all flesh is not the only one for the schools to follow. The world of Orwell's *1984* approaches, and Big Brother's approving chants of Doublethink threaten to make a mockery of schooling. The schools have a role to play and a chance in the struggle if teachers (and others into whose hands the young are brought) are themselves taught to use reason in education.

By way of acknowledgment, I wish to thank the members of the Commission on Publication of the Studies in Educational Theory of the John Dewey Society for their help and encouragement. Specifically, to Professor Robert E. Mason, its chairman, for laboring over the manuscript, offering suggestions, and encouraging me with unusual steadfastness. Professors Frederick Ellis and Ward Madden, also of the Commission, commented critically on the entire manuscript; and the latter, in particular, helped me to qualify my criticisms of Dewey and Raup (in Chapter III). My thanks also to Professor Israel Scheffler, of the Commission, for encouragement and enlightening criticisms, particularly on one of my sample arguments (early in Chapter I); and to Professor Joe Burnett, president of the Society, for continuing encouragement and helpful criticism of my argument in Chapter II.

Deep personal gratitude goes to Professor James E. McClellan, true friend and philosopher, who more than anyone else, I believe, taught me—if it can be taught at all—what it means to do a little philosophy. I am indebted to Professor Philip Phenix who, besides teaching me the importance of "vision" in philosophy of education, ingeniously showed me in an earlier version of this work why it is that not even truth-telling is under all conditions sacrosanct. Professor Arno Bellack, friend and mentor, drew my attention to actual problems of teaching and tried to keep me from the philosopher's trick of speculating too much about education in general. My gratitude to Professor Judith Jarvis Thomson for her most helpful comments on an earlier version (especially Chapters III, IV, and V), and, in particular, for suggesting a telling example of an overriding reason in education; and to Professor Sidney Morgenbesser, also for his comments on an earlier version and particularly for suggesting the rebuttal notion used in Chapter VI.

I am grateful to the following publishers and authors: The editors of the *Journal of Philosophy* for permission to quote from H. Broudy, "How Philosophical Can a Philosophy of Education Be?" Volume LII, No. 22 (October 27, 1955); J. E. McClellan, "Why Should the Humanities Be Taught?" Vol. 55 (November 6, 1958); and B. Othanel Smith, "Views on the Role of Philosophy in Teacher Education," Vol. LIX (October 25, 1962), and to these authors for granting permission to quote.

To Professor William R. Frankena for permission to quote excerpts from an unpublished paper, "McMurrin and Smith on the Philosophy of Education," read at the 1962 meeting of the Eastern Division of the American Philosophical Association.

To the University of Chicago Press for permission to quote excerpts from W. J. McGucken, "A Catholic Philosophy of Education," and H. Horne, "An Idealist Philosophy of Education," in the *Forty-first Yearbook of the National Society for the Study of Education,* 1942.

To Rand McNally and Company for permission to quote excerpts from Smith and Ennis, *Language and Concepts in Education,* 1961.

To the Syracuse University Press for permission to quote excerpts from Othanel Smith, "Basic Issues in American Secondary Education," in I. P. Halverson (ed.), *Frontiers of Secondary Education,* 1956.

To Prentice-Hall for permission to quote excerpts from H. Broudy, *Building a Philosophy of Education* (2nd ed., 1961).

To the editors of the *Harvard Educational Review* for permission to quote excerpts from S. Hook, "The Scope of Philosophy of Education", Vol. XXVI (Spring, 1956).

In writing this book, I benefited also from discussions with colleagues in the Department of Philosophy, both at the C. W. Post and Brooklyn Center branches of Long Island University. Thanks particularly to my friend and colleague at the Brooklyn Center, Alex Orenstein, for suggesting a biconditional statement designed to strengthen an argument (early in Chapter I).

My thanks also to the C. W. Post College of Long Island University for a small college research grant that defrayed the cost of preparing the manuscript for publication; to Mrs. Betty Hogan and Mr. Robert Demorest (the latter of the Ohio State University Press) for their valuable editorial help; and to Mrs. Jean Meeker for superb typing.

I happily dedicate this book to Elsie, my wife and true friend, who in so thoughtfully helping to bring up our daughter Nancy shows me in this and countless ways how vitally education can affect us all for the better.

BERTRAM BANDMAN

Long Island University
June 24, 1966

Table of Contents

Introduction 3

Part I: The Dilemma of the "Great Debate"

I. *The Two Senses of "Argument"* 9

II. *The Use of Metaphysical Arguments in Education* 43

III. *The Use of Moral Arguments in Education* 67

Afterword to Part I and Foreword to Part II 89

Part II: The Place of Reason in Assessing Educational Arguments

IV. *The Place of Metaphysical Reasons in Education* 95

V. *The Place of Moral Reasons in Education* 133

VI. *The Rebuttal Notion* 179

Index 195

The Place of Reason in Education

I grant that the tendency of the times is to exaggerate the good which teaching can do, but in trying to teach too much, in most matters, we have neglected others in respect of which a little sensible teaching would do no harm.

Samuel Butler

Introduction

Educational philosophies often collide without making much impact on the educational community. The inconclusiveness of such collisions may result from the absence of any court of appeal where arguments for or against educational proposals may be rationally assessed. This study seeks to clarify the relevance of philosophy to education through a philosophical examination of the crucial educational question "What should be taught?" Some of the main philosophical arguments purporting to answer that question will be evaluated in our quest for the constituents of good philosophical reasoning about what should be taught.

The purpose of this study is to determine *what, if anything, qualifies as a rational argument to help us decide what should be taught.* Are there any philosophical guidelines to help us assess an argument that is directed toward answering some form of the question "What should be taught?" Since there are usually at least two sides to an educational issue, the problem is to judge among opposing arguments and contradictory conclusions. (Issues, for example, might involve teachings for or against patriotism, for or against some sectarian belief, for or against a particular moral, political, or economic way of life.)

To implement the process of judgment, this study will search out philosophical canons of criticism by which alternative educational arguments may be assessed. Such canons of criticism are designed to provide a rational basis, comprising the necessary and sufficient conditions, for deciding what should be taught. There is no guarantee, of course, that these canons of criticism cannot, themselves, be criticized or even that these criteria answer all requirements. The aim here is really to sharpen our awareness of the need for competent criteria to do the job of appraising philosophical arguments in education. To this end, sustained effort will be made to distinguish a good reason from a not so good reason for deciding what should be taught.

First, it should be made clear that the question "What should be taught?" was prompted primarily by the importance to the philosophy of education of Plato's question "How ought we to live?" [1] and secondarily by the closely related educational question of R. M. Hare, "How shall I bring up my children?" [2] The belief is shared with Plato that a consideration of how we ought to live is no trivial matter; and the belief is shared with Hare that a consideration of how we ought to bring up our children is also of the highest philosophical importance. Some concentration on the question of what to teach may remedy the lamentable indifference, noted by Hare, that most philosophers since ancient times seem to have manifested toward the subject of how man should bring up his young.

This study will scrutinize philosophical arguments about the subjects to be learned, with a view to locating *the place of reason in education* (i.e., identifying the scope and limits of reason in education). If in searching for the place of reason in education pertinent canons of criticism can be found, they can be used to identify a rational argument and to refute as unacceptable an opposing argument. Relevant canons of criticism can also be used to distinguish among arguments worthy of attention and those deserving to be ignored or rebutted. Such criteria may not be able to furnish us with formal proof, but they could give us a gauge. If, however, applications of canons of criticism should actually be demonstrated as unsatisfactory or limited in usefulness, it would be edifying to know that, too. It is assumed here that it is possible to deal rationally with arguments used in educational controversy.

The intention here is not to impose any single philosophical standard upon the assessment of educational arguments. If a fixed formula for resolving an educational argument were presented, one might look upon this study as being like a book of etiquette or a style manual or an engineer's handbook, promising "the sure way" of doing something. The proposal here is less rigid and less simple—it is to turn to analytic philosophy for advice as to appraising evaluative arguments.

There is no promise that the advice will be either good or satisfactory. We may be left with sundry unresolved alternatives. Nevertheless, we need advice drawn from philosophical analysis, with a bearing on educational problems, more than we need injunctions deduced from philosophical doctrines that may be irrelevant to the problems of education. Let us explore, then, the possibility of finding some advice in philosophical analysis that may help us to determine a sound basis for judgment among contradictory educational arguments.

First, let us discover the obstacles. In Part One (Chapters I, II, and III), some main philosophical difficulties—specifically metaphysical and moral—are cited as obstructing the use of rational arguments to draw educational conclusions, generally, and to answer the question of what should be taught, particularly. Then let us surmount the obstacles. In Part Two (Chapters IV, V, and VI), some rational canons of criticism are presented for the assessment of metaphysical and moral arguments about what should be taught.

The attempt is made to criticize metaphysical and moral arguments in education, without either accepting or rejecting any philosophical doctrine *in toto*. This study does not advocate the abolition of metaphysics, nor does it urge the preservation of any particular metaphysical doctrine. The need to criticize metaphysical assumptions in education does not imply a wish to throw out the baby with the bath. Similarly, in moral philosophy, criticism is directed against even those positions that are too tempting to be discarded entirely. Following the example of J. W. N. Watkins, the attempt is made here to subject metaphysical and moral arguments in education to a maximal criticism of their unsatisfactory implications. The philosophical activity of so doing, without accepting or rejecting particular viewpoints *in toto,* may offer a way to assess alternative arguments concerning what should be taught.

The fruitfulness of this activity depends on the relevance and importance of this kind of philosophical criticism. What is known in analytic philosophy as an approach has influenced the modes of criticism used here, which are adaptations of principles and techniques of approach, not as a school of thought or movement, but as a way of doing philosophy. Philosophical analysis of this kind need not be either sterile or unilluminating, nor need it be irrelevant to the rational activity of appraising what should be taught.

1. F. M. Cornford (ed.), *The Republic of Plato* (London: Oxford University Press, 1945), 352D.

2. R. M. Hare, *The Language of Morals* (London: Oxford University Press, 1952), p. 74.

Part I. The Dilemma of the "Great Debate"

I. The Two Senses of "Argument"

Everyone who talks about education seems to agree that something is wrong with it. But few people agree on what the wrong thing is, and even fewer agree on how to set it right. A well-known philosopher of education writes:

> Education is something men argue about. Often it is praised; more often it is blamed for what happens to men and nations. The words "ought" and "must" pervade educational discussions, giving them an imperative and urgent mood. One feels that something can and should be done—presumably something different from what is being done.[1]

The one certainty is the clamor over the aims, content, and methods of education. Writers with widely divergent perspectives agree that there is major disagreement. Sidney Hook, for example, writes that "American education today is marked by confusion, uncertainty, and heated debate."[2] Paul Woodring writes that "we are engaged in a great national debate over the aims and purposes of education." [3] A recent book about schools is titled *The Great Debate.*[4] James Conant opens a recent book with a chapter called "A Quarrel among Educators." [5]

The debate is described on occasion in terms of war. Robert Hutchins concludes a book, *Conflict in Education,* with a chapter on "Education at War," [6] and another author opens her book with a chapter on "Education under Fire." [7]

The use of violent metaphors, the note of urgency, the emphasis on crisis—these symptoms are not missing from the writings of philosophers of education. Many a philosopher of education is susceptible to the hysteria that must by now be part of the initiation for beginning students of education. Theodore Brameld, a well-known philosopher of education, opens his book on educational philosophy with a chapter entitled "A Time of Great Debate"; and (perhaps to dramatize the social function of the philosophy of education) writes that "philosophy deals with matters of life and death." [8]

Despite the general agreement that there is a debate going on in education, it is difficult to discover just what all the shouting is about. Some writers and philosophers contend that the debate is and ought to be about the meaning and purpose of education. Others contend that the question concerns not the purposes of education, but the intellectual transformation of the content, organization, and method of teaching in various subjects and the political structure in which such transformation can best occur.[9]

James Conant, who has grown tired of debating the meaning or purpose of education, writes:

> When someone writes or says that what we need today in the United States is to decide first what we

> mean by "education," a sense of distasteful weariness overtakes me. I feel as though I were starting to see a badly scratched film of a poor movie for the second or third time. In such a mood, I am ready to define education as what goes on in schools and colleges. I am more inclined to examine present and past practices of teachers than attempt to deduce pedagogical precepts from a set of premises.[10]

In a similar vein, Martin Mayer writes:

> I had some sense of the unreality of the "great controversy" in education. The controversy has been entertaining to watch. The critic shouts that the schools are lazy and the educators are fools; the educators shouts back that the critics are reactionaries and their criticisms are ignorant and each can prove his case by quoting from the statements of the other. Both parties play before well-organized cheering sections: wrestling fans are not the only people who find relish in a fight when neither side fights fair.[11]

And about the aims of education, Mayer writes:

> It is well to rid oneself immediately of the business of "the aims of education." Discussions on this subject are among the dullest and most fruitless of human pursuits. Whatever the ideal general aims of education may be, they certainly cannot be accomplished in schools.[12]

Whether the debate is about the purpose or the content or the political structure of education or about something else may not be clearly differentiated, but it does seem reasonable to suggest that the debate fundamentally concerns the question of *what ought to be taught.*

All sorts of proposals are made in answer to this question. Some advocate more religion; others, more science; others, more mathematics; and still others, more attention to socialization. There is an endless diversity of courses proposed and opposed. One writer characterizes the controversy over the curriculum as a sort of St. Vitus' dance. Books, articles, and orations continue to flow over the problem of what ought to be taught. Yet little effort is made to settle the controversy by rational argument. Is the decision on what is taught a mere matter of caprice?

According to Israel Scheffler, the decision on what to teach need not be arbitrary. He writes:

> We do not . . . consider it a matter of indifference or whim just what the educator chooses to teach. Some selections we judge better than others. Nor [do] we . . . discuss issues of selection as if they hinged on personal taste alone. We try to convince others; we present ordered arguments.[13]

If there are such arguments, then how do they resolve the controversy over what should be taught?

How Are Educational Arguments Settled?

As an example of an educational argument, we may consider the following, by Robert M. Hutchins:

> Education implies teaching. Teaching implies knowledge. Knowledge is truth. The truth is everywhere the same. Hence, education should be everywhere the same.[14]

How do you assess an argument of this kind? Is the conclusion really proven, in the sense that it *necessarily* follows? Now we may consider a classic counterargument by Sidney Hook:

> Everyone needs to be healthy. . . . The definition of health is the same for all men. . . . But who will therefore deduce that all men must eat the same things . . . or exercise in the same way in order to be healthy? Just as there are different dietary roads to health, there are different curricular roads to educational maturity.[15]

One can question Hook's argument by trying to break down the analogy between education and eating or exercising. But does it break down? How does one decide which of these arguments is right?

It may be instructive at this point to test several criteria for usefulness in solving this problem. Let us look first at the formal logician's criterion. If formal logic would suffice to distinguish a good argument from a bad one in education, then we should have a rational criterion for accepting one educational argument instead of another. If distinguishing a logically valid argument from an invalid argument would not suffice, then we should have to look for a different criterion.

Many scholars are addicted to the notion that the final court of appeal in all things rational is formal logic. It is tempting to apply the formal logician's precise and elegant rules to messy or troublesome educational arguments and to pronounce the verdict in favor of those arguments that are amenable to the rules and against those that are not. But if the criteria of formal logic should not prove the case, it would be necessary to look for some less formal method of putting an argument on trial. To anticipate the position taken here, the formal ideal of logic will be found insufficient in some respects but adequate in others as a way of assessing educational arguments, and will not be altogether discarded.

Smullyan differentiates the validity, soundness, and rigor of an argument. An argument is *valid* when the premises logically imply the conclusion; the premises, if true, cannot logically imply a false conclusion. An argument is invalid when true premises imply a false conclusion. In addition to being valid, an argument is *sound* when its premises are in fact true. To be valid, an argument need not be sound, but an argument cannot be sound when it is not valid. Finally, an argument is *rigorous* when "it is correctly annotated." The annotation, though no part of the argument, is "a gloss or commentary, which explains the steps and cites the logical principles by which we may justify the advance from the premises to the conclusion of the argument." A rigorous argument must be valid. But a valid argument need not be rigorous "for it may not be annotated or its annotation may not be correct." According to Smullyan, logic "seeks to formulate the principles which are used in the construction and criticism of the annotations of arguments." Arguments are, finally, either conclusive or inconclusive; formal or logical arguments are conclusive, but empirical arguments are inconclusive.[16]

Difficulties arise when one attempts to apply these definitions to philosophical arguments about education. An argument must be valid and sound if it is to be acceptable, but one cannot always know whether the premises are true. Moreover, evaluative premises, required in an evaluative argument, are not generally regarded as either true or false. "Correct" annotation, which has to do with methods of gloss or commentary, is also difficult to ascertain because in philosophy, as in philosophy of education, there is no known correct method of annotation. Whether any educational argument can be rigorous therefore awaits philosophical study.

Do we consider that evaluative arguments in education follow the argument form? To what extent do educational arguments deviate from the standard argument form? Validity is a criterion for an educational argument in so far as the truth and falsity of its premises and conclusion are in question. When the premises are true in a valid argument, the conclusion is likewise true. When the premises are false and the conclusion is true, the argument may be valid—but it is not sound. For an argument to be both valid and sound, both the premises and the conclusion must be true.

The difficulty of applying the tests of validity and soundness can be seen in the following example:

> Subjects should be taught if and only if there is appreciable transfer of training.
>
> There is no appreciable transfer of training in Latin.
>
> ---
>
> Therefore, Latin should not be taught.

The minor premise is factual—empirically true or false. But the major premise is a value judgment and is therefore not empirically true or false in the same sense as a factual statement. The conclusion is an evaluative decision and therefore it also is not true or false in the empirical sense. When a premise and the conclusion of an evaluative argument in education are neither true nor false, how are we to apply the tests of validity and soundness?

In Smullyan's terms, rigor presupposes both validity and soundness. Rigor in a philosophical argument need not have these prerequisites, since one premise and the conclusion in a philosophical argument may be neither true nor false. But though a rigorous argument in philosophy or in the philosophy of education need not, strictly speaking, be either correctly or incorrectly annotated, the annotation of an evaluative argument (in education, at any rate) is nevertheless intended "to explain the steps and to cite the logical principles by which we may justify the advance from the premises to the conclusion of the argument." In both formal and evaluative arguments the attempt is made to *justify* one conclusion rather than any other (especially contradictory) conclusion. Thus annotation is focused on the type of evidence or reasoning adduced to buttress a conclusion.

We have seen that application of the validity and soundness standards to an evaluative argument cannot be done satisfactorily because evaluative statements are not either true or false. And there does not yet seem to be a satisfactory criterion for judging the rigor of an evaluative argument in education. How then can we choose between opposing arguments about what *should* be taught?

The field of education would be singularly blessed if there were a criterion (or set of criteria) for distinguishing a good educational argument from a poor one.

Idealized logic will not do it. An alternative, recently put forward by Stephen Toulmin, would relocate logic from the exclusive domain of mathematics to the arena of jurisprudential analogy for use in the critical assessment of actual arguments.[17] Logic, in its practical application, deals with the justification of conclusions.[18] Viewed as generalized rational criticism, logic is concerned with "the soundness of claims we make—with the solidity of grounds we produce to support them, the firmness of the backing we provide for them—or . . . with the sort of *case* we present in defense of our claims." Logic, then, is a kind of "generalized jurisprudence." [19]

Rules of logic are applied as standards of achievement whereby a man's argument can be judged. A sound, well-grounded argument measures up to standards and meets criticism. There is a notable difference between Toulmin's and Smullyan's notion of a sound argument: for Smullyan, the premises of a sound argument *must* be true; for Toulmin, they need not be true.

According to Toulmin, practical logic needs a "hypothetical bridge" to authorize an inference from a set of premises to a conclusion. To express this, Toulmin suggests a special formula or model (not entirely unlike some of Dewey's terminology) in which D stands for data or premises and C stands for the claim or conclusion. The bridge to authorize the inference from D to C is W, or warrant, a canon of argument.[20]

The practical logician's concern is the study of proper inferring procedures, that is, rational canons of inference. Logic, for Toulmin, is no "if-then" craft technique.[21] The logician is an argument assessor who does not apply invariant technical tests, such as one might to measure the endurance of metals, but must apply various rules to various types of argument.

Toulmin furnishes several examples for his models. Here is one of them: D denotes "Harry was born in Bermuda." W denotes "A man born in Bermuda is a British subject," authorizing the claim, C, that "Harry is therefore a British subject." The argument model looks like this:

$$D \longrightarrow \text{So } C$$
$$\text{Since } W$$

Since not all arguments are the same, Toulmin adds modal terms like N (for "necessarily") or P (for "probably") to qualify the claim. The qualifier, "if P," makes provision for exceptions, permitting the addition of degrees of force. Appealing to the legal analogy, Toulmin notes that some cases come directly under the law and others come under it with qualifications.[22] The features of ordinary arguments are made more complex than is the mathematician's ideal "Q.E.D." Added to the modal qualifier, Q, are the conditions of rebuttal, R, showing the circumstances under which a given conclusion or claim is liable to defeat (or, to borrow a term used by H. L. A. Hart, is made "defeasible"). While Q indicates the strength of W on the inferring step between the data and the claim, R indicates those circumstances that would set aside the otherwise general authority of W. R is, accordingly, capable of defeating the original claim, which is now prefaced "unless R." The revised model is then written:

$$D \longrightarrow \text{So } Q_1 \; C$$
$$\text{Since } W \text{ Unless } R$$

In the example, the conclusion that Harry is a British subject is now prefaced with the qualifier, "So presumably"; and the rebuttal condition, R, says, "Unless both his parents are aliens, or become naturalized Americans."[23]

Standing behind W, there is a certain backing, B, meaning in Harry's case "On account of the following statutes and legal provisions. . . . "

Toulmin distinguishes "field-invariant" from "field-dependent" factors in arguments: Q, R, W, and B are field-dependent because they vary from field to field, depending on the context and circumstances of argument; the inference from D to C, in its abstraction, is field-invariant.[24]

Note again how Toulmin's and Smullyan's views diverge. According to Toulmin, neither truth nor validity is a necessary criterion for soundness.[25] For Smullyan, both truth and validity are necessary for a sound argument.

Arguments are either analytic or substantial. Toulmin suggests that we abandon the analytic ideal because its criteria (truth conditions) are beside the point in dealing with substantial arguments.[26] He says we need criteria of appraisal for judging each field by its own relevant standards. In this connection, the traditional appeal to the analytic ideal tempts one to demand the mathematical logician's ideal to apply to arguments in practical fields, since some of his standards depend on the field rather than on mathematical logic alone.[27] There is no entailment in substantial arguments or the mathematician's ideal of validity in substantial arguments. Logic is not designed exclusively for the mathematician.[28] Validity, however, according to Toulmin, is an intrafield notion, not an interfield one. Toulmin calls for a comparative logic, comprising actual forms of argument current in any field. The starting point in this logic is admittedly empirical. Logic in the wider sense can be seen at work if one pays attention to substantive arguments, including their historical development in various fields.

One critic of Toulmin's use of arguments, John C. Cooley, points out that the Toulmin framework does not help us to decide between contradictory conclusions. According to Toulmin, (D) "Petersen is a Swede," (W) "90 per cent of all Swedes are non-Catholic" implies that (C) "Petersen is non-Catholic." Cooley sets up this counterexample: (D) "Peterson visited Lourdes," (W) "90 per cent of the visitors to Lourdes are Catholic." How does Toulmin's framework help us any more than dispensing with deductive framework and leaving to ordinary inductive procedures the decision as to whether Petersen is Catholic?

The Toulmin view is nevertheless an effective rejoinder to those (like Smullyan and Cooley) who hold that the analytic ideal will suffice as the sole method of performing all sorts of proper inferring procedures or of drawing sound conclusions in all kinds of arguments; for Toulmin draws attention to the problems that beset various fields and are not solved by applying the invariant standards of the mathematical ideal of logic to all sorts of non-mathematical problems. Toulmin does not deny the force and importance of formal logic. He reminds us, however, of a view recognized earlier by Mill and Dewey and alluded to still earlier by Aristotle that logic has also a larger, more general use—the rational appraisal of arguments in fields other than mathematics and science. Logic is not just formal; it is also informal, and practical as well as theoretical.

Which model or paradigm of argument should one use in assessing educational arguments? Smullyan and Toulmin provide different logical postures. Much of what follows will reflect an effort to take advantage of the strength of each stance in logic—the one too strict, the other, perhaps, too flexible. Formal logic, it seems, cannot be used alone to decide between contradictory evaluative arguments in education, nor can the scarcely visible strictures from actual arguments in education comprise an adequate guide.

Two senses of an argument might be distinguished. Formal logic, which rigorously demonstrates the conclusion, could be called "Sense II"; and "Sense I" could denote the special evaluative type of argument, which does not intend to demonstrate the conclusion, and is used in giving (probably inadequate) intellectual backing to decisions about "what should be taught." The following dialogues, F and E, may help to make the distinction:

F_1: 1. A is older than B.
2. *B is older than C.*
3. Therefore, A is older than C.

F_2: Yes, 1 and 2 are true, but I doubt 3.

F_1: All I can do is recoil at your remark.

Contrast that with the following:

E_1: There is no appreciable transfer of learning in teaching X; therefore, X should not be taught.

E_2: True, but there are other, overriding reasons for teaching X anyway, as follows: Y, Z.[29]

E_1: All I can do is recoil at your remark.

Here, E_1's final response is quite out of place; at any rate, it does not carry the logical weight of F_1's final response, which is in place.

There is no impropriety in either of these types of arguments, but one should not confuse them. On occasion an argument that looked at first like an E (evaluative) argument is suddenly treated as though it were an F (formal) argument. The conclusion of a formal argument is not debatable, not a matter of opinion; it is necessary. Empirical arguments, similarly, are not "mere" matters of opinion. To deny that fluorides help prevent tooth decay or to assert that there is an appreciable transfer of learning in declaiming Latin verbs is simply to be unenlightened. Nevertheless, educational discussions are sometimes carried on without careful attention to the pertinent factual evidence.

Confusion of evaluative argument with formally demonstrable argument is caused, in part, by the philosophers of education who present their views as forcefully as possible (as will subsequently be illustrated). The strong determination of educational philosophers to present ironclad arguments for their conclusions makes their efforts resemble those of the legal advocate who wishes, similarly, to have an ironclad case. Educationists and philosophers of education advocate contradictory conclusions, much as lawyers do; and two contradictory conclusions cannot both be right.

A special philosophical difficulty seems to occur when philosophers of education, using an evaluative argument of the type of Sense I (not intended to demonstrate conclusions), suddenly assert a conclusion as though it were derived from a formal argument. Sometimes an argument that begins in the manner of Sense I seems to move by nearly imperceptible degrees out of Sense I and into Sense II. The resulting difficulty is reminiscent of Hume's observation that philosophers often speak for a while as though their propositions were built on some form of "is," only to confront one suddenly with "no proposition that is not connected with an *ought* or an *ought not*." [30]

Thus far alternative models of argument forms have been sketched. The question is how they will work in deciding what should be taught. Smullyan and Toulmin cannot both be right, one asserting that true premises are a necessary condition for a sound conclusion, and the other that truth is not a necessary condition for a sound argument. Each appeals to a different type of language—Smullyan to the technical logician's language, Toulmin to the less precise, more elastic language of the lawyer, for whom truth and validity are not, in every case, the necessary criteria for sound argument.

One must know what constitutes a sound argument in education in order rationally to appraise alternative answers to the question of what should be taught. If true premises and validity are not to be our criteria, what will be?

To anticipate, the attempt will be made to show that Smullyan's paradigm, ideal as it is for the logician, will not, for several reasons, be suitable for the evaluative inference in which educationists engage when they try to decide what to teach. The attempt will also be made to show that Toulmin's interpretation of arguments is not suitable as a criterion for use in deciding what to teach. The principal contention will be that, whereas Smullyan's notion of a sound argument is too taut, Toulmin's is too loose. From both views, we can hope to draw some appropriate advice later on how to appraise an educational argument; but neither model of argument will, itself, provide us with our needed criterion.

How Do Educational Arguments Answer Educational Questions?

The difficulty of resolving or settling educational arguments may be seen by examining the way philosophers of education answer their own questions in contrast to the way mathematicians or physicists answer theirs. One writer in philosophy of education notes this relationship between question and answer in connection with the question "Why should the humanities be taught?"

> There are some questions that can be answered by a simple affirmation or negation, others that can be answered by a proper name or statement. But "Why should the humanities be taught?" requires an argument for its answer, a set of premises fitted to some assumed logical model in such manner that they constitute good reasons for assenting to "The humanities should be taught.[31]

This study concerning the kind of argument required to answer the question "What ought to be taught?" will concern itself first with kinds of questions.

Isaiah Berlin and some other English philosophers have distinguished among formal, empirical, and philosophical questions. This distinction, which will be adopted here, is based on the different methods involved in answering these three kinds of questions. (For the purposes of this discussion, moral, metaphysical, and other philosophical questions are included in the rubric of "evaluative" questions.) The three questions "Is the word 'cat' a three-letter word?", "Is there any gold in the Sahara?", and "Is it good to spank children for thumbing their noses at adults?" are examples, respectively, of formal, factual, and evaluative questions. (A similar distinction is made by Renford Bambrough between "inquisitive" and "deliberative" questions. "Where is the nearest telephone booth?" is an example of the first; "Shall I vote Labor or Conservative?" is an example of the second. Techniques of proof or evidence are used to answer inquisitive, that is, formal or factual, questions, whereas techniques of persuasion are used in answering deliberative, that is, evaluative, questions.)[32]

Of formal, factual, and evaluative questions, the evaluative are the most troublesome. Although such factual questions as "What are the boundaries of the universe?" and "What is the cause of cancer?" may have no answers, there do exist techniques of proof or evidence that would enable us, should the occasion arise, to cry "Eureka!" We generally know what conditions must obtain in order for us to answer a formal question. We know, for example, that "forty-two" is the answer to the question "What is six times seven?" We know this by knowing the system of numbers in which six, seven, and forty-two are formally related.

An empirical question is clearly answerable, in the sense that we know what conditions must obtain in order to find the answer. We know, for example, that "the Empire State Building" is the answer to the question "What is the tallest building in the world?", and we know that the conditions for the answer are the measurement of the relative height of buildings. Similarly, we can answer a factual question in education, such as, "Does the teaching of driving in high school result in a decrease of juvenile traffic fatalities?" We answer this, as we do all other factual questions, by examining the pertinent evidence.

Thus a question in mathematics or in science can usually be considered answerable in that conditions indicate the necessary procedures and criteria for obtaining the answer. But with an evaluative question, the conditions for answering do not appear to be as plain as those for answering a formal or factual question.

The difficulty is illustrated by Herbert Spencer's question "What knowledge is of most worth?" Educators of differing persuasions acknowledge the significance of this question. They even agree that if we knew what knowledge is of most worth, we would know what to teach.

Herbert Spencer answered the question as follows:

> Thus to the question we set out with—what knowledge is of most worth—the uniform reply is—Science. That is the verdict on all counts. For direct self-preservation, or the maintenance of life and health, the all important knowledge is—Science. For that indirect self-preservation which we call gaining a livelihood, the knowledge of greatest value is—Science. For the due discharge of parental functions the proper guidance to be found is to be found only in—Science. For that interpretation of normal life, past and present, without which the citizen cannot rightly regulate his conduct, the indispensable key is—Science. Alike for the most perfect production and present enjoyment of art in all its forms, the needful preparation is still—Science, and for the purposes of discipline—intellectual, moral and religious—the most efficient study is once more—Science.[33]

Father William J. McGucken also asked the question "What knowledge is of most worth?" He answered it as follows:

> This question the Catholic answers in straightforward fashion: religious knowledge, knowledge of God and man's relation to God as made known through reason and revelation—that is the knowledge that is of most worth. Not that the Catholic schools of any type are concerned merely with knowledge of Christian doctrine. The point is academic; it is conceivable that in a more

> primitive civilization some Catholic schools might confine themselves almost, if not exclusively, to religious knowledge. The thing to be insisted on is that religion permeates all Catholic education from arithmetic to zoology, just as ideally it impregnates all of Catholic life and living. Naturally, there is no such thing as Catholic chemistry; yet in a chemistry class taught in a Catholic school to Catholics by a Catholic, there will be an awareness of and a reverence for God and supernatural values. The Catholic scientist will never make the mistake of becoming so absorbed in test tubes that there is no room for a higher loyalty.[34]

If S (Spencer's question) had meant to ask, "What knowledge (do you think) is of most worth?", then it would be like a question intended in Sense I, such as, "How do you feel about peach pie?" In that case, Spencer could have his answer and Father McGucken his, and neither would be wrong. But if S did not mean to ask, "What do you think? . . . " (or, "How do you feel? . . . "), then S would be more like a question intended in Sense II, such as, "What is the tallest building in the world?", which can be answered by reference to measurements. Interpreting Spencer's question as having the intention of Sense I seems specious. We sometimes seem to have in mind an intention other than Sense I when we ask S—an intention that seeks an answer at least more like Sense II than like Sense I.

The Catholic answer is X; some other group (Lutheran, Idealist, Marxist, Experimentalist, etc.) may answer Y, which is logically incompatible with X. The problem is: How do we answer such a question? If one man says X and another says Y, who is right? How do we choose between X and $\sim X$ as the answer to the question "What knowledge is of most worth?"

To the question about the tallest building, someone answers, "the Woolworth" (or W); and someone else says, "the Empire State Building" (or ~ W). We can readily settle this question because we do have a way of choosing between W and ~ W. But how do we choose between X and ~ X in answer to S? Can we say Spencer's question is "answered" when we give the Catholic or some similar reply to it? Or does the very presence of opposing answers to an educational question of this sort constitute the answer to the question?

It would be very satisfying if we could determine the "correct" answer to an evaluative, educational question with as much facility as we do the answer to a formal or factual question. But as we have seen, in response to the question "What knowledge is of most worth?", Spencer has his answer and Father McGucken has his; and we have no way of knowing which is right.

How we answer an educational question may depend on what we mean by the word "answer." "Answer" need not be limited to the sense in which "George Washington" answers the question "Who was the first President of the United States?" To say, "George Washington was the first President of the United States," gives a true answer to that question. Call it Sense II. Consider Sense I, in which the answer "There are bodies and minds, as well as relations between bodies and minds governed by a Deity," may be given to the metaphysical question "What is there?"; other answers might be given to that question. There are logically incompatible answers to the same question. Thus, to the questions of what and how to teach, Hutchins gives his answers and Dewey gives his, just as to the question "Whom shall we teach?", segregationists give one answer, desegregationists another. The two sets of answers are logically incompatible or inconsistent with each other because we cannot put both sets of answers into action simultaneously. (Of course, if A says, "My answer is X.", and B says, "My answer is Y.", little difficulty arises so long as neither A nor B intends to assert that X or Y is *true.*) But these two uses of the word "answer"—sometimes as a synonym for "response" or "reply" and at other times as a synonym for "solution" or "true statement"—are not always clearly distinguished, nor is the word "answer" used in all cases in only one sense. Answers to formal and factual questions are usually capable of being tested as true statements or solutions, but answers to philosophical questions do not seem open to similar tests. Philosophical questions, then, are not answered in Sense II but in (or more like) Sense I.

The distinction between these senses is important enough for further elaboration. When your telephone rings and you lift the receiver to reply, you may be said to answer the telephone in Sense I, even though what you say in answer to some question may be utterly false. If an answer is false, or neither true nor false, then the question has *not* been answered in Sense II. If, however, a question is answered in Sense II as a "true statement" or as "the correct solution to a problem," it is self-contradictory to say that it is the wrong answer or a false answer, for it cannot be both "true" and "false" or "wrong." While it is in order to say of an answer in Sense I, "X answers the question, but X is wrong," it is logically odd to say of an answer in Sense II, "X answers the question, but X is wrong." What serves as an answer in Sense I does not necessarily serve as an answer in Sense II.

An answer in Sense II must do more than satisfy the condition of truth. If it is to be taken as cognitive, an answer in Sense II must also satisfy the further conditions of relevance and credibility.[35] If an answer in Sense II were required to satisfy only the condition of being a true statement, the following dialogue might occur:

A: "What's your name?"

B: "My kitten is a small cat."

C: "That's no answer."

D: "According to the above condition of what counts as a cognitive answer, it is. It's a true statement, isn't it?"

A: "Well, I'll be . . . "

An answer in Sense II fulfils the following three conditions of a cognitive statement:

1. It is true.
2. It is believed.
3. It is relevant.

(The concealed phrase "do you think" in "What knowledge is of most worth?" may be shown to lack relevance, when we distinguish our two senses of "answer." Without that phrase, the question is presumably intended to be answered in Sense II.)

We may also speak of Senses I and II as the "intentional" and "successful" uses (respectively) of the word "answer." Although these are not, strictly speaking, the same as "response" and "solution" in the question-answer relation, a successful answer is a solution to a problem or question; an unsuccessful answer may "intend" to solve the problem but is no solution. (Note how this distinction can be applied to the so-called Final Solution of the Jewish Question, which, had it been successful, might well have been the factual answer to the question "How to exterminate European Jewry?" The moral ignominy of the phrase "final solution" in such a context does not affect the factual propriety of that phrase, given the depraved moral setting and background of the Nazis.)

Not every response, however intended, is successful. This distinction roughly parallels Ryle's distinction between "task" and "achievement" words as well as Scheffler's distinction between "task" and "achievement" uses of words. In this case, the word "answer" may be used for either. That is, the intentional sense does not imply the success sense. And yet these two senses of the word "answer" (sometimes as a synonym for "response," sometimes as a synonym for "solution") are not always clearly distinguished. Consequently, the use of the word in Sense I ("response") slides imperceptibly into its use in Sense II ("solution"). Yet a philosophical question is often asked with the intention of obtaining, as the result of asking and of some form of proof or demonstration, a *true* statement as an answer. This may be called the dilemma of the philosophical question.

A question may be asked either with or without the intention of obtaining a true answer. If we do not care whether the answer to our question is true, our use of questions can only serve the view that ours is an Alice-in-Wonderland world where there are no true answers known (or knowable) to questions and no sensible reasons for asking questions (such as to find out what is true or to decide what is the right thing to do).

If, on the contrary, we set out to arrive at true answers to our questions, but find others saying that *their* answers—which are logically incompatible with ours—are true, we have contradictory answers. How are we to find out which of several logically incompatible "true" answers is true?

We may have too many answers, none of which is intended to be regarded as true—a situation in which any answer is as good (or as bad) as any other. Or we may have just two logically contradictory answers, with no way of choosing between them. Either situation makes philosophical questions, deep and interesting though they may be, fundamentally futile.

This seeming dilemma of the philosophical question is shared by questions in the philosophy of education. Here problems of education—such as what, how, and whom to teach—urgently demand solution, with proper consideration for philosophical rationale. Here the point in asking an important question is to get, in answer, the same sort of (true) statement that we use in answering the question "Who was the first President of the United States?" But our many answers are of the Sense I type.

Will answers of the Sense I type do for evaluative questions? If questions in philosophy of education do have answers, are they like the answers to "How do you feel about peach pie?" or like answers to "Is peach pie nice?" Will we not have a conflict among answers, one of which contradicts another? Now, there is no contradiction in "I like peach pie" and "I don't like it"; but there is a contradiction between "Peach pie is nice" and "No, it's not," unless one adds "for me" or "in my opinion." Is the "do you like" form characteristic of questions in education? Not quite. Questions in education are asked with the intention of being answered in quite another sense, or so it seems. For example, are questions like Counts's "Dare the school build a new social order?", Spencer's "What knowledge is of most worth?", or Brameld's "Where are we going?" [36] intended to obtain answers more like Sense I or like Sense II? Not altogether like Sense I, apparently. Both Counts and Brameld try to show, partly in polemical fashion and partly through a dialectical argument, what the answer is; they also make clear their belief that no other answer, especially its contradictory, will do. Brameld's philosophy can be interpreted as his own detailed answer to his question "Where are we going?" He clearly intends that, among the four alternatives—Perennialism, Essentialism, Progressivism, and Reconstructionism—we should choose the last, for among these alternatives this alone offers a worthy guide for the process of education.

Here, then, is the rub. Brameld, Counts, Spencer, McGucken—and, perhaps, almost all other philosophers of education—intend their answers to be true or somehow right; yet the test question for all of them arises: Does this answer succeed? How can any one answer succeed when there are so many, and among them some, at least, are clearly incompatible and competitive with the others? If one answer can succeed, which one is it, and how are we to tell?

The method of proof or evidence exists to check the correctness of an answer to a formal or factual question, but there is no similar method for answering philosophical questions (in Sense II). One writer notes that "we find it hard to answer such questions, and if a philosopher propounds one answer, another philosopher offers a different one." He adds, "What is worse, we do not know how to choose among various answers." [37] A recent writer in educational philosophy expresses the same difficulty in this way: "One man's metaphysics is another man's nonsense, and where there is a dispute among metaphysicians or theologians, particularly on moral concerns, there is no court of appeal to which we may repair to settle the question." [38]

A philosophical question may be asked with the intention of being answered in Sense I, causing no basis for misgiving. But sometimes a question in the philosophy of education that is asked in Sense I (seeking response) is answered with a shift of ground to Sense II (solution). The shift may be only dimly apparent, but it seems (to adapt a remark of Hume's in a similar connection), "of the last consequence."

For each man to say that *he* has the *true* answer to the main philosophical questions is somewhat ludicrous, especially when he has no way of showing conclusively that those who disagree with him are wrong. The effect of a steady stream of such answers, each claiming infallibility, is to give every answer (intended in Sense II) a somewhat will-o'-the-wisp air.

The absence of a court of appeal—of a standard for choosing among rival answers, each of which intends to be taken in Sense II, and each of which has its own source of authority—presents problems of caprice. An answer intended to be taken in Sense II, when rival answers make the same claim, and when there is no universally accepted standard for choosing among them, is not a responsible "answer." If there is no standard, then Spencer, McGucken, and others have their various answers; while each intends his to be accepted as true, so long as there are no criteria as to what counts (in Sense II), and therefore no basis for choice, the title of "answer" can only be used capriciously. It is not that McGucken or anyone else intends his answer to be taken so. It is simply that until a standard for settling philosophical questions is established, capriciousness will continue to be a chronic condition of philosophical questions and answers generally—Spencer's and McGucken's and all others of that kind.

The question-answer dilemma in philosophy and in philosophy of education lies, then, in intending or purporting to give answers (in Sense II) without having standards to justify the exclusion of opposing answers.

We have what may be called the Purist versus the Capricious use of the word "answer."[39] The Purist use is based on a strict standard of the sort used, for example, by those who support the Verification Principle; by and large, this is the standard used to arrive at answers to factual questions, such as, "What is the tallest building in the world?" The Capricious use of the word "answer" occurs in relation to certain disquieting philosophical questions—moral, metaphysical, and epistemological—and also in relation to troubling questions in philosophy of education. Here, for example, Spencer can "answer" the question "What knowledge is of most worth?" in one way, while Father McGucken "answers" this very same question in quite another way.

The difficulty with the Purist use of the word "answer" is that it invokes an idealized standard, a counsel of perfection that is inapplicable to those truly difficult and important educational questions that come before us, such as Spencer's. The Purist use eliminates philosophical answers altogether—Spencer's as well as McGucken's—as "meaningless"; it admits indicative assertions only. The Purist use of "answer" is of no more help here than is the Capricious. Both are employed in this study to illustrate caricatures; neither will do to guide our choice of answers to evaluative questions in education.

We may, however, consider something from each of these two uses. The Purist use provides an example of what an idealized answer would look like, even though the idealized answer that does not apply to our educational questions does us no good. A counsel of perfection may just be too remote to settle our questions. Yet we cannot have pedagogic chaos (witness educational debates), with no way to bring order from among competing answers.

The comments on the two uses of "answer" may be applied to the different uses of argument in the field of education. The use of argument, for example, by formal logicians like Smullyan seems to be rigorous and yet overly restrictive. A less restrictive use of argument certainly occurs in the courtroom, the strategy room, in labor-management relations, domestic and foreign negotiations, in national and international forums, and, perhaps, in every area of human discussion.

Because the Smullyan ideal is overly restrictive, it cannot be used to differentiate good and bad evaluative arguments in education. Since evaluative premises are not either true or false, *all* evaluative arguments, in Smullyan's view, are without exception unsound. If we were to apply Smullyan's idealized standard, therefore, there is no evaluative argument that would not have to be judged unsound.

The Purist criterion thus seems to exclude many arguments, metaphysical and moral, that ought to be included; the Capricious use of argument, by contrast, includes many arguments that we should have some way of excluding, and yet we have none. Whereas the Purist use of argument would indiscriminately eliminate all evaluative arguments in education, the Capricious use of argument indiscriminately admits them all. The Purist, in short, eliminates too much; the Capricious admits too much. It follows, then, that neither the Purist nor the Capricious use of argument provides a satisfactory basis for judging evaluative arguments in education.

Is the Purist ideal altogether impossible of realization? Is it only a mathematical logician's dream? Lest one think that the logician's restrictive criteria for rational argument amount to a counsel of despair (as to some educational arguments), one should note that the Purist use of argument provides a formally desirable example of univocity and a model of a satisfactory argument. The Purist use does not, however, furnish any criterion for deciding which evaluative arguments in education to heed and which to ignore. It is consequently of little direct practical help to us.

Shall we settle for "democracy" among arguments? Shall we unharness ourselves from the Purist use of argument, only to be saddled with the Capricious use? Is nothing, after all, to qualify as an evaluative argument that may finally put Spencer's type of question to rest? Is there no way out of the impasse between the Purist and the Capricious use of argument?

In the chapters to follow, whether or not we find a way out of the Purist-Capricious impasse, we may begin to discern what counts as a rational argument in answer to the question "What should be taught?" The challenge, to sum up, will be complex. Apparently we must adopt either the Purist or the Capricious use of "argument." The Purist conception of the word, which would exclude *every* evaluative argument as "unsound," is too restrictive to be a criterion for judging arguments in the philosophy of education. The Capricious conception, on the other hand, would admit any argument at all. We are at an impasse as long as we attempt to adopt *either* of them for deciding questions about what to teach.

Besides the Purist and the Capricious uses, is there some other use of the word "argument" that may eliminate the difficulty inherent in either? What, specifically, counts as a rational argument to answer the evaluative question of what should be taught? Or, more generally, *what is the place of reason in education?*

The solution, if there is one, may consist in suitably modifying and applying both the Purist and the Capricious ideal to assess evaluative arguments in education. Adapting a famous remark of Kant's, educational arguments without any standards (say, arguments in philosophy of education) are blind; and a standard that does not take account of the use of evaluative arguments in education is empty.

Our predicament is this: Educational philosophy depends on the use of arguments; we have seen some of the arguments, and we have also seen that, to settle them, we need a standard or criterion for choosing among rival arguments. We can *respond* to educational arguments, if we will, in our different ways (Spencer's or McGucken's, etc.); but that will not settle the arguments, in the sense of providing a *solution* or rational settlement. A criterion must allow for formal and factual arguments and for evaluative ones too.

The philosophy of education is in need of a rational criterion (or set of rational criteria) to guide our choice among contradictory evaluative conclusions. A satisfactory criterion, if there is one, will give us rational grounds for accepting some evaluative arguments and rejecting others.

The remainder of Part I of this study will seek out some main philosophical difficulties—specifically metaphysical and moral—that lie in the way of using rational arguments to answer the question of what should be taught; Part Two will employ rational canons of criticism in assessing metaphysical and moral arguments to be used in deciding what should be taught.

This study has attempted, at the start, not to prove which of several contradictory arguments in education is valid or sound but, instead, to note the difficulties that are encountered in drawing an evaluative conclusion in education. In this, the effort has been made to follow the example of George Edward Moore who, in a similar connection, wrote:

> . . . With regard to the question "What ought we to do?", I have endeavored rather to show exactly what is the meaning of the question and what difficulties must consequently be faced in answering it, than to prove that any particular answers are true.[40]

1. Harry S. Broudy, *Building a Philosophy of Education* (2d ed.; New York: Prentice-Hall, 1961), p. 3. Copyright © 1961. Prentice-Hall, Inc., Englewood Cliffs, N. J.

2. *Education for Modern Man* (2d ed.; New York: A. Knopf, 1963), p. 8.

3. *One Fourth of a Nation* (New York: McGraw-Hill, 1957), p. 6.

4. C. Winfield Scott, Clyde M. Hill, and Hobert W. Burns (eds.), *The Great Debate: Our Schools in Crisis* (Englewood Cliffs, N. J.: Spectrum, 1959).

5. James Bryant Conant, *The Education of American Teachers* (New York: McGraw-Hill, 1963).

6. Robert Maynard Hutchins, *Education for Freedom* (New York: Grove Press, 1963).

7. Mary Anne Raywid, *The Ax-Grinders* (New York: Macmillan, 1962).

8. *Philosophies of Education in Cultural Perspective* (New York: Henry Holt, 1955), p. 19.

9. Solon T. Kimball and James E. McClellan, Jr., *Education and the New America* (New York: Random House, 1962), pp. 20, 27, 39.

10. James Bryant Conant, *The Child, the Parent, and the State* (Cambridge: Harvard University Press, 1960), p. 1.

11. *The Schools* (New York: Harper, 1961), pp. iii, xii.

12. *Ibid.*, p. 30.

13. "Justifying Curriculum Decisions," *School Review*, Winter, 1958, p. 461.

14. Robert Maynard Hutchins, *The Higher Learning in America* (New Haven: Yale University Press, 1936), p. 5.

15. "Modern Education and Its Critics," in Israel Scheffler (ed.), *Philosophy and Education* (Boston: Allyn & Bacon, 1958), p. 282. See also E. R. Emmett, *Uses of Reason* (New York: Longmans, 1960), pp. 225–26, for a further criticism of Hutchins' argument.

16. Arthur Smullyan, *Fundamentals of Logic* (New York: Prentice-Hall, 1962), pp. 2–4.

17. Stephen Edelston Toulmin, *The Uses of Argument* (New York: Cambridge University Press, 1958), p. 3.

18. *Ibid.*, p. 6.

19. *Ibid.*, p. 7.

20. *Ibid.*, p. 98.

21. *Ibid.*, p. 4.

22. *Ibid.*, p. 101.

23. *Ibid.*, p. 101.

24. *Ibid.*, p. 15.

25. *Ibid.*, p. 125.

26. *Ibid.*, p. 234.

27. *Ibid.*, p. 250.

28. *Ibid.*, p. 250.

29. The logic of either the F or E argument is formally impeccable and the same in that sense, that is, that either the F or E argument is valid. But there is a question concerning the soundness of the argument. When E_2 says "True . . . ," he refers to the factual premise (2) that in X there is no transfer of training, but not to the evaluative premise that is not said to be true in the same sense that (2) is said to be verified as a true statement.

By inserting a wedge into the argument, that is, in not accepting the major premise as the only consideration for deciding upon (3), E_2 is able to get out of having to acquiesce to the conclusion (3). F is a formal argument; E, in addition to being formally arguable, is also arguable on (what Toulmin calls) *substantial grounds.*

If the major premise stated that only subjects in which transfer of learning was present should be taught, then E_2's remark concerning admissibility of "other overriding reasons" would be out of place. To make this point clearer consider this further example in place of E_1: (1) Important subjects should be taught. (2) Latin is important. (3) Therefore, Latin should be taught. If "only" is tacitly assumed in (1) and prefaces "important" and if (1) and (2) are true, then (3) follows necessarily. There is then no difference (formally) between F and E. But in fact there is disagreement about (1) in E_1 that is absent in (1) in F_1. To make this point still clearer, if one prefaces (1) and (2) in both E and F examples with "if," then there is no difference between E and F; but in *actual usage* debate is liable to occur about (1) in E_1 that is not as frequently liable to occur about F_1. Recoiling is out of place in E because rebuttals in which overriding reasons are given are in place. One could counter the second example in E by saying: (1) Only the more important subjects should be taught. (2) Greek is more important than Latin. (3) Therefore, Greek should be taught instead of Latin. Or, in the E_1 example, it could be that "transfer of learning" is not the only reason for teaching a subject, that the contribution of a subject to understanding of Western culture *is a more important reason* for teaching it than its transfer of learning to other subjects.

In E and F the formal aspects of the argument are the same; but in the actual usage of evaluative arguments, unresolved disagreements may arise concerning the truth or rightness of the evaluative premise that are not so apt to arise over the major premise of a formal argument. In a formal argument the premises are tacitly prefaced by "if" clauses, e.g.: If A is older than B, and, If B is older than C, Then A is older than C. If, in addition, the argument is used empirically, then the truth of each of the premises can be verified and one can say, "Ah, *but* didn't you know that A is really not older than B." Similarly, if in addition to formal considerations, an argument is used evaluatively, then the evaluative premise may not be used with an understood or assumed "if." In an evaluative argument of the kind E, there is room for a wedge in which "but" clauses take the place of "if" clauses.

30. L. A. Selby-Bigge, *Treatise on Human Nature* (Oxford: Oxford University Press, 1906), Book III, Part One, Section i.

31. James E. McClellan, "Why Should the Humanities Be Taught?", *Journal of Philosophy,* LV (November 6, 1958), 998.

32. Bambrough has used deliberative questions in two different articles to distinguish in turn between metaphysical and moral questions: "Gods and Giants," *The Listener* (July, 1965); and "Plato's Political Analogies," in F. Laslett (ed.), *Philosophy, Politics and Society* (New York: Macmillian, 1956), pp. 112–14.

33. *Education: Intellectual, Moral and Physical* (New York: A. L. Burt Co., 1859), pp. 63–64.

34. "The Philosophy of Catholic Education," *Forty-first Yearbook,* National Society for the Study of Education (1942), p. 279.

35. This practice of answering a question in philosophy of education is by no means confined to McGucken. H. Horne, for example, says: "Idealism as a philosophy has its characteristic answer to all the main questions about our world. What is it to be? Or what is being? . . . To what is the order of the world due? The order of the world is the problem of cosmology and Idealism holds that the order of the world is due to the manifestations in space and time of an eternal and spiritual reality." "An Idealist Philosophy of Education," *Forty-first Yearbook,* National Society for the Study of Education (1942), pp. 139–40.

36. Brameld, *op. cit.,* p. 464.

37. Abraham Kaplan, *The New World of Philosophy* (New York: Random House, 1961), p. 94.

38. Van Cleve Morris, *Philosophy and the American School* (Boston: Houghton-Mifflin, 1961), p. 361.

39. For a related view see Abraham Kaplan, "Are Moral Judgments Assertions?", *Philosophical Review,* LI (1942), 280–303.

40. *Principia Ethica* (New York: Cambridge University Press, 1903), p. 276.

II. The Use of Metaphysical Arguments in Education

How a metaphysical argument is used in the philosophy of education often depends on how the word "argument" is used. An argument in education (as we noted in Chapter I) may plead a case as a trial lawyer does or may express a verdict as a judge does. This advocacy-verdict distinction, suggested in another connection by Nowell-Smith in his *Ethics,* resembles the response-solution distinction between the Sense I (response) answer to a philosophical question in education and the Sense II (solution) answer. The resemblance is modified importantly in so far as a verdict may be wrong and still be a verdict, but an answer or "solution" in Sense II that is wrong is no longer an answer. Although the suggestion by Nowell-Smith may thus be closer to Toulmin's jurisprudential paradigm than to the response-solution distinction, a verdict is, in a sense, impartial by assumption. A similar distinction is seen in the two senses of the word "argument," which we sometimes call "persuasion" and sometimes call "demonstration." The "intend-succeed" distinction used in discussing certain verbs is also seen, with qualification, in Senses I and II of "answer" and "argument."

An argument may be used at first in Sense I, in order to persuade, to plead for a position, to express advocacy, and then may be changed in treatment to Sense II, as though it were being used to render a verdict. This, again, may arouse misgiving.

Such an argument may be said to be concluded in one sense when it is actually being concluded in another. A form of the *reductio ad absurdum* (similar to that used by Ryle) can test an argument purportedly concluded in Sense II as to whether it was indeed concluded in that sense.

Spencer's conclusion in answer to the question "What knowledge is of most worth?" is one of many examples of the difficulty of concluding an argument, when one has the intention of concluding it noncapriciously. The following metaphysical questions have been asked in philosophy of education by Harry Broudy:

> Are there any truths about the world, about man or about goodness, that are universal, eternal and valid for all men in all circumstances? If so, then do not these constitute the basis for a fixed curriculum . . . ? Or is all this talk of truth (and eternal values) moonshine? Is truth relative, like the weather or the Dow-Jones averages and the peculiarities of our ancestral superstitions? If so, then does not the newer school with and for the individual to develop his own truth and his own destiny seem the logical and sensible alternative?[1]

The problem (as with Spencer's question) is *how* one answers such questions as: "Are there any truths . . . ?" "Do not these constitute the basis for a fixed curriculum . . . ?" "Or is all this talk about truth moonshine?" Which kind of argument will do? If one man says X and another says Y, who is right?

Has any answer in Sense II been found? It would seem not. It is with this difficulty in mind that consideration will now be given to how an argument is used to answer a metaphysical question in education.

Educational Definitions

Several kinds of arguments are used to "answer" metaphysical questions in education (like those raised by Broudy). One kind uses *definition* to give conceptual clarification to puzzling terms or expressions.[2] This use seeks conceptual clarification of such terms as "religion," "education," "method,"[3] "learning," "experience," "mind," "professional," "theory," "discipline," and expressions like "the logical order of knowledge," or "meeting the needs of youth," or "equal educational opportunity."

One may, for example, seek a conceptual clarification of religion that is intended to bear on the question of whether religion shall be taught. In clarifying the concept of religion, one may make a distinction between teaching about religions and indoctrinating on behalf of a religion (or teaching people to be religious).[4] Or one may argue that clarification of the concept of religion must make the religious experience intellectually defensible. Or one may argue that religion is a private and solitary experience, not subject to argument or refutation.[5]

But a booby trap is concealed in efforts to answer questions by clarifying concepts in philosophy of education. Inherent in these efforts lies the limitation that the device of a shift from a metaphysical argument to a conceptual analysis may clarify the issue but does not *settle* it. This method does not answer questions in Sense II. In philosophy of education, a residual question remains after conceptual clarification,[6] and that is: Which among competing usages shall be adopted?[7] The shift from an argument that is out-and-out metaphysical to one that is conceptual may clear the ground a little, but it does not dispose of the deliberative question. The philosopher of education still has to make up his mind which usages among competing concepts (although clarified) he shall adopt. This question remains as to "religion," "educational theory," "curriculum," "method," "excellence," "the logical order of knowledge," "equal educational opportunity," and "meeting the needs of youth."

The limitation of conceptual clarification may be most dramatically illustrated in the debates over social and political terms such as "democracy," "states' rights," "civil rights," and "social change." These debates, hedged around with arguments in defense of various proposed usages, still leave open the question of which usage ought to be adopted.[8] One can see the deliberative aspect of conceptual studies and definitions in education, which intend to coax, goad or guide, inspire, move—in short, to get educationists *to act*. This kind of definition is akin to the persuasive defintions described by Charles Stevenson, which were used to persuade someone to think or act in the way intended by the speaker.[9]

Definitions in the field of education are important means of clarifying concepts and problems, even though they do not settle them. On occasion, however, an educational definition purportedly settles a difficult issue, as if it had the nature of a conclusive argument. Mortimer J. Adler, for example, writes:

> The philosopher of education is primarily concerned with the educational ideal, with answering the question, "What is the best education absolutely for any man according to his essence?" This is the problem he solves by defining the ultimate ends . . . as the absolute and universal principles of education. . . . This can be proved.[10]

G. E. Moore cites the source of the paradox of attempting to prove an argument by definition:

> One man says a triangle is a circle. Another replies: "A triangle is a straight line, and I will prove to you that I am right, for a straight line is not a circle." "This is quite true," the other may reply: "but nevertheless a triangle is a circle and you have said nothing whatever to prove the contrary. . . . Which is wrong, there can be no earthly means of proving, since you define a triangle as a straight line and I define it as a circle." [11]

The same difficulty occurs when one tries to answer the question "What is education?" with a definition. Hutchins answers, "Education is the cultivation of the intellect"; Dewey answers, "Education is growth." Although, for either Hutchins or Dewey, education is not at all what the other says, neither of the two has any earthly means of proving which is right. (A similar difficulty occurs in attempts to settle by definition the question "What is man?" [12] Hence, an educational definition (being nonreportive, whether it be persuasive or programmatic)[13] can be used by anyone to suit his own purposes.[14] A metaphysical argument that is "settled" by definition is, accordingly, an argument only in Sense I and not in Sense II.

The foregoing criticism of definitions is not intended to deny their importance but solely to point up one use of definitions that is inadequate (for the reasons cited) to demonstrate conclusions in education. (See Chapter IV for a further consideration of educational definitions.)

Metaphysical Beliefs

In addition to the efforts to settle metaphysical arguments in education by means of definition, attempts to settle them are made even more commonly through whole systems of beliefs or isms, such as Realism, Idealism, Thomism, Marxism, or Experimentalism.[15] A metaphysical belief or ism is used by some philosophers of education to answer a metaphysical question, such as, "Are there certain truths and principles which hold for all times and places" [16]; or, "Can man live adequately in time without thought of Eternity?" [17]; and also to imply answers to such educational questions as "What shall be taught?"

Since the use of implication is prominent in educational arguments, one may well consider how, or in what sense of "implication," a given philosophical position can "imply" conclusions for education.

According to one prominent writer, Professor Harry Broudy, either the derivative or the constructive approach[18] is usually used to show how a metaphysical belief implies answers to educational questions.

According to the derivative approach, conclusions for education are deduced from a given philosophical position. According to the constructive approach, educational issues rise to successively higher grounds of argument, until, finally, they reach the last court of appeal—metaphysics—beyond which there is no rational means of resolving unsettled educational questions. A philosophy of education is thus built up from consideration of educational questions that cannot be settled by either emotive of factual appeal. Such questions are taken to the philosophical, including the metaphysical, level for resolution. Professor Broudy, who uses this approach, avers:

> As we seek the answers to a number of educational issues, it will become clear that we have to resort to views about reality, about knowledge, about goodness, and about beauty, and what views we have about these may determine our choice in these practical issues.[19]

According to the constructive approach, educational questions that are not settled on an emotive, factual, or theoretical level become philosophical questions. These questions are answered by metaphysical beliefs or isms, which in turn imply answers to practical educational questions.[20]

In Broudy's view, the derivative approach consists in answering the question "What does a given position imply for education?" On this basis, Sidney Hook charged that "to encourage philosophers, as Mr. Broudy does, to derive [a philosophy of education] from some philosophical position such as Idealism, Realism, Thomism, Pragmatism, or Existentialism is to encourage them to perpetrate garrulous absurdities." [21] Professor Joe Burnett thereupon responded to Hook's contention with the observation that while this is one way in which philosophy of education works, Broudy does not necessarily endorse the practice. Burnett said that "following almost immediately on the heels of this expression to which Hook refers," Broudy pointed to some serious logical difficulties involved in attempting to derive educational principles and practices from a philosophical position. Broudy indeed holds:

> Logically, it may be impossible to make more than plausible guesses, because educational theory takes into account existential factors that have the brutishness of particulars and do not necessarily follow any principle. Thus Thomist educators do not agree on which methods or even which type of curriculum would be implied by a curricula seem to be compatible with that philosophy.[22]

Yet Broudy then says:

> Instrumentalism comes off best in this type of derivation. Whatever difficulties and shortcomings the derivative method . . . may harbor, to carry it on . . . demands a high order of technical competence both in philosophy and education. The mental processes used in effecting the derivation, moreover, are indistinguishable from those used by philosophers *qua* philosophers.[23]

This hardly sounds as though Broudy regards such derivation, "the milking of a philosophical position for its educational implications," as a logical impossibility or in any way disclaims the value of the derivative approach. As Broudy says:

> Whatever the merits of these methods (the derivative and the constructive), the contention of this paper is that they can qualify as philosophical, both with respect to content and method.[24]

Moreover, between the very heels that Burnett spoke about, one finds two sentences. The first reads: "Philosophical points of view may imply much or little for education." Whether it is little or much that a philosophical position or ism implies for education, this sentence does not at all deny that a philosophical position has implications for education. The second sentence reads: "Every position implies at least the value of studying and stating that position, and to that extent would favor an education that would encourage such study and statement." [25] If Broudy means that the advocates of each ism believe that their position is worth studying, then the advocates of a position may believe either (1) that it is worthwhile for themselves to study it, or (2) it is worthwhile not only for advocates, but also for many or all others, to study the position, or (3) it is worthwhile for others to *adopt* the position.

As to (1), how could advocates of a philosophical position believe in it without thinking it worth their while to study and know something about it? Broudy apparently does not intend to deny (1). But to assert (1) is tautological, trivial, and hardly interesting.

While (2) includes mention of (1), it says also that it is worthwhile for others to study the position, meaning that the position *should* be studied by others. But should *all others* really study a given philosophical position? This has certainly not been shown; more is implied in the conclusion than there is in the premises. Concretely, Thomism or Marxism (*et al.*) may imply the value of teaching that doctrine either to Catholics or to Communists (assuming a definition of teaching). But to suggest that Thomism ought to be taught to others or to everyone (either historically, as a way of life chosen by millions for nearly two thousand years, or persuasively, as a way of life to which others should be converted), adds more to the conclusion than there is in the premises. Such a suggestion is a clear-cut case of using a particular premise to "imply" a universal conclusion (a violation of the logical rule that there cannot be more in the conclusion than there is in the premises).

Moreover, the contention that a philosophical position implies the imperative that it should be studied is again a case of implying more in the conclusion than there is in the premises.

A comparable difficulty is cited by Anthony Flew. To say, "God wills X" does not imply that "one ought to obey God's will." "One ought to obey God's will" is needed as an additional premise in order to imply that one ought therefore to do X.[26] To say that "Thomism says X" similarly does not imply that one ought either (2) to study or (3) to follow Thomism. The additional premise "One ought to study (or follow) Thomism" is needed, if one wishes to imply that one ought therefore to study or follow it. But Broudy nowhere suggests this among the logical difficulties of deriving an educational conclusion from the statement of a philosophical position. The implication in (3), of course, is even more extreme than in (2), for (3) commands us to *follow* or to *embrace* an ism. Broudy is surely aware of the difficulty of implying (3) since, among the isms, one could not simultaneously embrace rivals. At any rate, the tenor of his article indicates that he does not wish to suggest the third alternative. But this difference between (2) and (3), while affecting the assumed definition of teaching, does not diminish the logical difficulty of choosing (2), since either one concludes more than is included in the premises. So much, then, for the derivative approach.

Broudy prefers to use the constructive approach. Broudy's question "*What* [italics added] does a given position imply for education?" proposes that a given position imply an answer to a set of practical educational questions like, "Shall religion be taught as part of general education?" Broudy adds the following qualification: "Although the starting point of the discussion was an educational problem" (whether to back religion or to expand college education), "and its terminus, it is to be hoped, will be an educational solution, the discussion *both in content and in method* [italics added] will be throughout philosophical." [27]

This approach still means either that an educational program based on the principles of a given philosophical doctrine shall be taught to those who already share the same belief or that the same program should be taught to many others or to all. Use of a metaphysical belief or ism to imply answers to evaluate questions (whether one prescribes or proscribes the teaching of religion as the conclusion from a philosophical position) is no different from use of the metaphysical belief that "God made us and therefore has an absolute claim on our obedience" to imply that we ought "to do and be what He desires." [28]

According to D. J. O'Connor:

> It is not possible to deduce statements about the aims of a system of education or its curriculum from any purely philosophical statements. This follows from an obvious extension of Hume's principle . . . that the evidence for any conclusion must contain statements of the same logical sort as the conclusion itself.[29]

Whether we go from education to philosophy or come to education from philosophy, it is on philosophy that Broudy relies to settle practical educational controversies,[30] such as, "Shall religion be taught as part of general education?" [31] To begin with, avers Broudy, the physical and social sciences provide factual evidence to answer this sort of practical question. But the controversies involved "cannot be decided by facts." Questions of fact are settled only "when agreement on norms or objectives has been achieved." Broudy states:

> If, therefore, the controversy is to continue in rational fashion, both parties will have to take the issue to a higher level. Each position will have to be justified in terms of value schemata which, in turn, depend on epistemological, ethical and metaphysical theory.[32]

On the question of religion, for example, Broudy says:

> The issue as to whether religion should or should not be a part of general education, can be stated in economic, sociological, political or psychological terms to begin with, but sooner or later it has to be fought out on epistemological grounds. Either the religious categories have truth value or they do not . . . for unless the educator can have superior knowledge in these matters, his claim to autonomy and authority is empty.[33]

Similar educational issues also have "to be fought out" on philosophical grounds and settled, if at all (that is, when every other rational or evidential recourse fails), philosophically. What, then, is the difference whether a philosophical position implies answers to basic educational questions or the educational questions rise to be "fought out on epistemological grounds"?

With either approach, a philosophical statement is used to imply an answer to an evaluative question in education. To deduce "statements about the aims of a system of education or its curriculum from purely philosophical statements" commits the fallacy, long ago noted by Hume, of deriving what ought to be from what is. This fallacy is more than a matter of grammar; it is a matter of a conclusion that contains more than there is in the premises.

Broudy may not abstain from deriving answers to educational questions from philosophical positions such as Idealism, Realism, Pragmatism, or Existentialism. The derivative and constructive approaches go around the same circle, even though apparently in different ways. Whether a philosophical position "implies" answers to educational questions or educational answers must be derived from a philosophical position makes no essential difference because both routes lead to the difficulty, raised by the open question, of using a philosophical position or an ism to determine evaluative conclusions for education.[34]

It is possible that Sidney Hook is guilty of the very "crime" he accuses Broudy of committing, encouraging philosophers "to derive (a philosophy of education) from some philosophical position."[35] How does one answer Hook's question "What are the ends of education?" If the answer is not to be sought in metaphysics or epistemology, where then? Assuming that it is found in ethics or social philosophy, the values are either derived or underived. If they are underived, how do we justify them? If they are derived, how do we derive them? Though derivation "is no easy task," says Hook, "it involves detailed study of the biological, psychological, and historical nature of human beings, their culture and traditions and focal problems, in short, anything which is relevant to settling" the question,

"What is of worth in human life?" [36] But are such concepts as " 'Being is one' or 'Being is many,' 'God created the world' or their denials" irrelevant to Hook's question "What is of worth in human life?" And are they irrelevant on Hook's own grounds of study, especially culture, traditions, and focal problems?

According to Hook, an answer to the question "What are the ends of education?" follows from an answer to the prior question "What is of worth in human life?" How does one answer this prior question? Does the detailed study that he describes exclude philosophy, particularly epistemology or metaphysics? Whatever Hook's objections to transcendent metaphysics, attention to such concepts as "Being is one," etc. is surely not irrelevant to all the studies involved, even though it may not *imply* anything about these studies. Hook uses this conclusion, "A philosophy of education will develop when philosophers and educators . . . concern themselves with questions of education, explore their bearing on conflicting value commitments and seek some comprehensive theory of human values to guide us in the resolution of conflicts," [37] to answer the question "What is of worth in human life?" and hence to answer the question "What are the ends of education?" But on what grounds does his conclusion exclude any consideration of the metaphysical concept "Being is one" or its denial? What makes metaphysics irrelevant to all the fields of study that he mentions, especially culture, traditions, and focal problems, as well as the biological, psychological, and historical nature of human beings? What makes metaphysics irrelevant to his conclusion that involves a "comprehensive theory of human values" in answer to the question "What is of worth in human life?" and finally to the question "What are the ends of education?"

Hook may dislike Broudy's derivative approach, but he has one of his own—from the fields of study to the conclusion that answers first the "human life" question and thus the "education" question. The conclusion uses studies that supposedly exclude philosophy for answering the questions. But is it not apparent that Hook derives a philosophy of education from a philosophical ism, Pragmatism (rather than Realism or Idealism, etc.)? Witness the language of the study areas, the conclusion, the exclusion of metaphysics. Does he not continue—in his own particular fashion—precisely what he condemns in Broudy and others? This is nowhere so evident as in his concern about derivation in others. Yet neither derivation, his or that of others, escapes the open question, the fallacy noted by Hume.

In the derivative or the constructive approach (or in disclaiming them), when one uses a metaphysical belief to imply conclusions for education, one is confronted by the open question of how something can be in the conclusion—an educational "ought"—that is not in the premises. The trouble with the "isms" approach is that its inevitable reduction to a particular doctrine leaves us with a philosophical particular used to imply a universal conclusion. Thus, whether one adopts the derivative or the constructive approach (or denies doing so), a metaphysical argument in education may properly be used in one sense but not in another.

The sort of educational implication that falls outside the four known kinds of implication—formal, definitional, causal, or material—[38] is indeed a curious sense of "implication." How can one characterize this save as persuasive?

Just as a persuasive definition[39] expresses a favored usage of a word and exhorts others to adopt that usage, so a philosophical position may imply persuasively or programmatically a favored curriculum that one exhorts others to favor. While a persuasive definition is used occasionally to propose an illuminating distinction, so a philosophical position may be used to distinguish one sort of justification for a curricular proposal from some other. Each ism makes a distinction by attempting to show that it offers the best way to educate, both because of its curricular program and because of its justification, which answers the question of why that particular curriculum is proposed.

Persuasive or programmatic implication expresses the intent of implication in philosophy of education. The intent is not logical implication because this implication is not formal, nor definitional, nor causal, nor material, nor really any sort of implication at all; the intent is *justification* of an educational conclusion. What is being asked all along is not "How does the philosophy of X *imply* educational conclusion Y?", but "How does the philosophy of X *justify* educational conclusion Y?" What is stated reads: Ism X *implies* "Teach Y"; what is intended, however, is: Ism X *justifies* the demand "Teach Y." There lies the heart of the problem.

The question arises: Is the ism a rationalization, or is it a philosophically adequate justification capable of implying, albeit persuasively, a curricular program? The answer has to be shown for each case; on the heels of it steps a second question, "Does this answer succeed?" Does the ism justify a given curriculum as the best and, on those grounds, support the claim that it should be taught to everyone? If the answer to the second question is negative, then the open question that we have seen in the two preceding cases is confronted again.

The question "*What* does a given philosophical position imply for education?" may now be restated, "*How* does a given philosophical position imply conclusions for education?" (That is, "In what sense does the philosophy of X *imply* answers to basic educational questions such as 'What shall we teach?', 'How shall we teach?', 'Whom shall we teach?' " The restated question no longer asks, "*Does* a given philosophical position imply conclusions for education, and if so, what conclusions?" but, "*How* does it imply conclusions?" One significant difference is that while the question "Does X imply Y?" is answered by "Yes" or "No," the question "*How* does the philosophy of X imply conclusion Y for education?" is answered by argument. If the answer to the question "Does X imply Y?" has been "Yes," one can and must ask the "*How*" question, "*In what sense of 'imply'*?"

Although the question "How does X imply Y?" may seem to lack the advantage of leading to an answer that tells us once and for all whether X implies Y, it has an important advantage of drawing attention to the meaning or manner of implication. There may, in the end, be more found out by asking "How?" than by asking "Whether?" "How?" demands some form of demonstration or argument for justification. Furthermore, in the process of showing *how* X implies Y, *what* X is finally shown to imply may turn out to be the same as though nothing (cognitive) were being implied at all. In that case, we would have a perfectly legitimate method of refutation (a *reductio ad absurdum*), without thereby prohibiting to educationists (whether they are for or against metaphysics) the use of the persuasive sense to draw practical conclusions for education.

Deeper questions are pressing. The purpose of studying the question "How does a given philosophical position (the philosophy of X) imply conclusions for education (that we should teach Y)?" has been to show that although a metaphysical argument, derivative or not, may *intend* Sense II, a persuasive implication *cannot succeed* in concluding a metaphysical argument in that sense.

A metaphysical argument in education is said to be settled by an educational definition or by a metaphysical belief. Either way, an argument is given—although not in the sense of "argument" that is being sought. A metaphysical question answered either by definition or by metaphysical belief is answered in the persuasive rather than the demonstrable sense of argument. Two approaches, the derivative and the constructive, show how metaphysical beliefs are used to "settle" educational arguments. With both, however, the philosophy of X can only be said to imply an argument to answer Y in one sense, although quite another sense of "answer" is being sought.

Examination of metaphysical arguments in education illuminates an obstacle to "settling" such arguments that perhaps was formerly not recognized. The effort has been made to show the essential difficulty that arises when they are "settled" by definition or belief. In either case, misgiving arises when the sense of intent in the word "argument" is shifted to the sense of success ("solution" [40] or "conclusion"). (If one supposes that one has established the certainty of one's conclusion to an educational argument, in the sense that one establishes the certainty of an answer or solution to a question, then one is misapplying an educational argument in one of the senses of "argument" that does not in fact apply it. This indistinguishability between two senses in some philosophers' minds tempts one to repeat Wittgenstein's remark that "one can only stammer about such things.")

Understanding how a metaphysical argument answers a metaphysical question may keep Horne's question "Can man live adequately in time without thought of Eternity?"; or Heidegger's question "Why is there anything at all?"; or Broudy's question "Are there any truths or principles for all times and places?", from seeming to be foolish, meaningless, unanswerable, or unarguable—so long as one does not confuse one sense of an argument with another.

The mite that may be thrown into the receptacle as a contribution to the proper evaluation of metaphysical arguments in education is this: We have neither to affirm nor to deny that the arguments noted settle metaphysical questions, but we have rather to show, in each case, *how*—whether in Sense I or Sense II. The metaphysical argument in education, for all that it may seem to be used in or like Sense II, is really used more like Sense I.

Metaphysics may in the foregoing sense imply conclusions for education. Noteworthy, however, is that educational definitions and metaphysical beliefs occasionally take on the character of arguments that are Capricious rather than Purist; they are more like persuasive definitions and persuasive implications than like demonstrable arguments, principally because there is more in the conclusion than there was in the premises. The special difficulty with educational definitions and beliefs is that, in being reduced to particular doctrines, they become particular premises used to imply universal conclusions. Thus metaphysical arguments using educational definitions and beliefs are apt to be more like Sense I than Sense II. Is there no way out of the Sense I and Sense II dilemma? Are all our arguments more like Sense I than Sense II? The attempt has been made to reveal that there are no standards for judging metaphysical arguments in education.

The next chapter turns to moral arguments in education to see what, if any, distinctive difficulties they may place in the way of drawing conclusions in education.

1. H. S. Broudy, *Building a Philosophy of Education* (2nd. ed.), p. 18. Copyright © 1961. Prentice-Hall, Inc. Englewood Cliffs, N. J. It should not be construed from this that Broudy answers his metaphysical questions in as cavalier a fashion as either McGucken or

Horne. Quite the contrary. In arguing for the philosophy of Classical Realism as the answer to these questions, he repeatedly qualifies his use of "answer" or "solution." But skilful and adroit as Broudy's answer is, like Spencer's answer, it, too, does not come off in Sense II. Hence both Spencer and Broudy, like other philosophical builders, have fallen victim to a philosophical dilemma.

2. Analytic philosophers in education have been predominantly concerned with the clarification and consideration of the use of terms and expressions. See, for example, B. Othanel Smith and Robert H. Ennis (eds.), *Language and Concepts in Education* (Chicago: Rand McNally, 1961).

3. For a philosophical clarification of method in education, see James E. McClellan, "Dewey and the Concept of Method: Quest for the Philosopher's Stone in Education," *The School Review,* LXVII (Summer, 1959), 213–28. The argument concerning method is shown in its relation to the metaphysical issue of the one and the many; and both in metaphysics and method the penchant for oneness is held futile, as this study in conceptual analysis of method sets out to show.

4. See, for example, Israel Scheffler, *The Language of Education* (Springfield, Ill.: Charles C. Thomas, 1960), pp. 100–101, in which Scheffler distinguishes the ambiguous phrase, "the teaching of religion" into a teaching-*that* (the fact-stating component in teaching that a given religion consists of such and such "historical institutions, doctrines, attitudes") and teaching someone *to be* religious. One may favor the "teaching of religion" in either sense while consistently opposing it in the other. "To be clear about debates over religion in the curriculum requires elementary clarity with respect to the construction to be put on the phrase 'the teaching or religion.' "

5. For a discussion of this approach, see Morton White, "Religion, Politics, and Higher Learning," in Israel Scheffler (ed.), *Philosophy and Education* (Boston: Allyn & Bacon, 1958), p. 244.

6. Perhaps akin to the "open texture" F. Waismann discusses ("Language Strata," in *Logic and Language,* Second Series, ed. A. G. N. Flew [Oxford: Basil Blackwell, 1953] pp. 11–31) in an effort to show how the meaning of terms can and cannot be exactly tied down—a sort of Heisenberg indeterminacy or underdefinability principle.

7. For example, one writer clarifies the concept of an educational theory by comparing it with a scientific theory; showing that educational theory comes off badly in this comparison, he argues for the usage of "educational theory" as a "courtesy title."—Daniel J. O'Connor, *An Introduction to Philosophy of Education* (London: Routledge and

Kegan Paul, 1957), pp. 92–110. Another writer argues that, because educational theory is to be autonomous, the comparison between educational and scientific theory is invidious; that educational theory can effectively guide educational pratcice, even though it is value-neutral with respect to philosophical systems. (Foster McMurray, "Preface to an Autonomous Discipline of Education," *Educational Theory,* V [July, 1955], 129–40.) Still another aims to make clear the function of educational theory by showing that it is not nearly so independent of philosophical systems or value-neutral. (Joe Burnett, "On Professor McMurray's Autonomous Discipline of Education," *Educational Theory,* VII [January, 1956], 18–21.) The controversy as to what it means for theory to guide practice continues more recently with other controversialists entering the fray, viz., D. Bob Gowin and H. Perkinson in *Educational Theory* (1964). "Science," "discipline," and "profession" are other terms about which philosophers of education argue. The intent seems to be to show education in analogy with science, profession, or discipline, to exhibit a preferred usage in a good or favorable light.

8. A deliberative question is one answered by a recommendation often expressed with the word "shall," as in "We shall adopt policy X" or "We shall teach Y in our school system." The "shall" question in philosophy of education asks for an argument to show that one *ought to* adopt this definition (or purpose) rather than that, for example, Dewey's definition of education rather than Hutchins' or vice versa. The educationist's arguments may not be rationally convincing, but they are meant to be as attractive as possible, with a view to enticing members of the teaching profession to adopt a similar belief. But this is no exhortation, pure and simple, for the appeal made need not be wholly extra-rational. See Part Two for a further elaboration of how imperative or deliberative conclusions or decisions in education may be to some extent at least rationally buttressed. (See also my article, 'On the Fundamental Question of Ethics," *Mind,* LXXIV [January, 1965], No. 293.

9. See Charles Stevenson, "Persuasive Definition," *Mind,* XLIX (1938), 339–40. The intent of a persuasive definition is to use a term in a certain way, so as to evoke either a laudatory or derogatory attitude. To suggest, for example, that Plato's "Republic," or the Soviet Union, or the state of Mississippi is a "closed society," is intended to evoke a derogatory attitude toward them. A persuasive definition may also, however, make an insightful comparison or distinction hitherto unnoticed, as, for example, the one-time (now recognized to be overstated) remark "Metaphysics is nonsense," or "The meaning of a statement is the method of its verification." Or, to apply this to education: "Teaching without learning is meaningless." See also Scheffler,

The Language of Education, Chapter I, especially pp. 20–21; and Komisar and McClellan, Preface to the American Education, in C. D. Hardie, *Truth and Fallacy in Educational Theory,* especially p. xv, in which they argue that philosophical analysis of educational terms, contrary to the charges of some of its critics, is intended to eventuate in moral guidance and prescription. "It is the educator's occupational mandate to culminate his work in recommendations."

10. Mortimer J. Adler, "In Defense of the Philosophy of Education," *Forty-first Yearbook,* National Society for the Study of Education (Chicago: University of Chicago Press, 1942), pp. 221–29.

11. *Principia Ethica,* p. 11.

12. For a related discussion, cf. O'Connor's criticism of Maritain's question "Who are we?" in which Maritain is said to offer "disguised conclusions of argument on natural religion and very debatable ones at that."—*An Introduction to Philosophy of Education,* pp. 115–18. For a paradoxical discussion, see Adler (*op. cit.*), in which he asserts that the one true philosophy of education can be demonstrated only if all symposiasts affirmed the undemonstrable truths of metaphysics and the nature of man; but since they disagree, "they should not pretend to give, nor the readers expect to get, demonstrations" (p. 204).

13. Scheffler, *The Language of Education.* See Chapter I for a discussion of programmatic definitions and how they compare with persuasive definitions. Scheffler attempts to stress the cognitive import of programmatic definitions (p. 20): "Programmatic definitions raise moral issues" and, in particular, "they may be used to express serious moral choices" (p. 21). If one man defines eductaion by saying, "Education is a process of adjustment to life experiences" and another says, "Education is the cultivation of the intellect," a moral choice may very well be expressed; but if the one argues for X and the other for Y in this way, does the definition decide anything that warrants our calling it "cognitive"?

14. See B. Othanel Smith and Robert H. Ennis, *op. cit.,* p. 86. "It is well understood that words can be defined to satisfy the purpose of the individual who uses them. For this reason, many controversies center on the meaning of terms. The literature of education is filled with claims and counter-claims about the meaning of 'education.' One authority defines education as growth; another says it is the cultivation of intellectual virtues; and still another claims that education is the means by which civilization is transmitted from one generation to another. These definitions are controversial, because each one is packed with a set of preferences about what is to be taught, how it is to be taught, who is to be educated, and so on. And conducting the

controversy consists in unpacking the definitions, each side pointing out what to include, and at the same time claiming its own conception to be more defensible and desirable."

15. See, for example, the *Forty-first* and the *Fifty-fourth Yearbook,* National Society for the Study of Education.

16. See H. Broudy, "A Classical Realist's View of Education," in Philip H. Phenix (ed.), *Philosophies of Education* (New York: John Wiley, 1961), p. 21.

17. H. Horne, "Twenty-three Years Later," in Joe Park (ed.), *Selected Readings in the Philosophy of Education* (New York: Macmillan, 1958), p. 193.

18. For a fuller account, see Harry S. Broudy, "How Philosophical Can a Philosophy of Education Be?", *Journal of Philosophy,* 52 (Oct. 27, 1955), 615–18; also his *Building a Philosophy of Education* (1961), p. 13.

19. H. S. Broudy, *Building a Philosophy of Education* (2nd ed.), p. 19. Copyright © 1961. Prentice-Hall, Inc., Englewood Cliffs, N.J.

20. Two yearbooks in the philosophy of education and, in particular, the work of Professor Harry Broudy, a charge by Sidney Hook, and a response by Professor Joe Burnett clearly show the use of "implication" in metaphysical arguments in education.

21. Sidney Hook, "The Scope of Philosophy of Education," *Harvard Educational Review,* XXVI (Spring, 1956), 148.

22. "How Philosophical Can a Philosophy of Education Be?" p. 617.

23. *Ibid.*, pp. 617–18.

24. *Ibid.*, p. 618. The following qualifications needs to be noted carefully. A metaphysical premise X logically implies an educational conclusion Y, only in the sense that Y is consistent with X. For example, Hutchins's emphasis on intellectual virtue would not stress a life-activities type of curriculum, and Dewey's emphasis on growth makes it inconsistent to endorse, to stress, and to put into practice a "St. John's University Great Books" type of curriculum. All that is at stake is whether what is proposed is consistent with a metaphysical belief. Thus it would, for example, be inconsistent if Hutchins, who believes in "the cultivation of the intellect" in the classical tradition, were to propose an educational curriculum which emphasized "life-adjustment" experiences, which interfered with the study of the Great Books. But, since Hutchins proposes the teaching of the Great Books rather than life-adjustment experiences, his educational pro-

posal may be said to be logically implied (in addition to other premises) by his belief in the development of the intellect.

25. *Ibid.*, p. 617.

26. See Anthony Flew and Alasdair MacIntyre (eds.) *New Essays in Philosophical Theology* (New York: Macmillan, 1956), pp. 101–8.

27. *Op. cit.*, p. 617.

28. See O'Connor, *An Introduction to Philosophy of Education,* p. 128.

29. *Ibid.*, p. 106.

30. Broudy's use of philosophy seems to make philosophy out to be a tribunal or Supreme Court, a function one would think philosophy had lost during this century.

31. Broudy, "How Philosophical Can a Philosophy of Education Be?", p. 616.

32. *Ibid.*, p. 615.

33. *Ibid.*

34. A metaphysical belief does not imply an educational policy at least in this sense: that a metaphysical belief can be used to *sanction* both of two incompatible policies. Further, divergent and incompatible metaphysical beliefs do not necessarily imply incompatible educational policies. An example of the first: agreement on the belief in God does not necessarily *resolve* a disagreement concerning the teaching of reading. Nor, as an example of the second, does disagreement about the existence of God necessarily *imply* disagreement concerning the method of teaching reading.

35. Hook, "The Scope of Philosophy of Education," p. 146.

36. *Ibid.*

37. *Ibid.*, p. 148.

38. Irving Copi, *Introduction to Logic* (New York: Macmillan, 1961), pp. 245–48.

39. For an account of persuasive definitions in education, see Scheffler, *The Language of Education,* Chapter I.

40. Note that Broudy hopes that philosophy will bring about a solution to an educational problem. He does not say that philosophy *does* do so, although the hope that it does result in a *solution* may be a vain chimera, one no longer sought even in analytic philosophy.

III. *The Use of Moral Arguments in Education*

A metaphysical belief (a belief in a transcendent God or in a naturalistic world) may be invoked as an ultimate basis for decisions about what, how, or whom to teach. A philosophical position is claimed, on this ground, to "imply" practical conclusions for education. One difficulty in the appeal to metaphysical belief for implication of educational policy decisions is the kinship of educational argument to persuasive rather than to demonstrable argument. This permits a conclusion to appear on occasion as the "proven" conclusion of a metaphysical argument, while the argument is actually "concluded" only in the persuasive sense and not at all in the demonstrable sense.

Practical educational conclusions may be drawn from moral beliefs as well as from metaphysical beliefs. The effort to justify an educational program may be solely and overtly moral. Witness, for example, Sidney Hook's conclusion to an educational question where he tries to avoid involvement with metaphysics.

The dependence of curricular proposals on moral beliefs is not hard to see. Education is designed to be of some particular service to the society that creates it. The goals and values of a society are believed relevant to the ends of education—which in turn guide, if not imply, practical educational policies and programs. Reference is made, often glibly and inexactly, to "culture" as a basis for deciding the ends, contents, and means of education. The inescapable fact of the existence of a culture makes it impossible to deny altogether its goals and values that are meant to serve as the ends of education. The question is, *which* goals and values of the culture shall determine the ends of education?

The appeal to this sort of justification is sometimes metaphysical and sometimes moral. Different traditions have different and often conflicting concepts of what the ends of education should be. It may be meaningful to consider how a moral argument is used in the philosophy of education (whether such an argument is more nearly "persuasive" or "demonstrable").

The effort to use a moral argument in philosophy of education runs up against the hurdle of drawing a valid ethical conclusion—a condition made plain by R. M. Hare, and before him by G. E. Moore. The problem is, in effect, that what *ought to be* cannot validly be deducted from what *is*. If "is" implied "ought" or "right," one could substitute "is" for "ought" or "right," and say, "What is, is right"—which is not necessarily the import when one says that something is morally right. It would be self-contradictory—substituting "is" for "ought"—to say, "X is so, but X ought not to be so." [1] One could not take moral exception to what actually happened. In a world where "is" equaled "ought," one could argue from "Hitler killed six million Jews" to "Hitler was right." Similarly, one could point to an instance of segregated schooling and say, "See, that proves it's right." The method would be the same one that is used in observing the height of buildings; but it would not be possible to argue the case one way or the other or to deny what was morally wrong if "is" actually meant the same thing as "ought." A satisfactory conclusion to a moral argument must at least be a validly derived "ought" statement.[2]

Several recent efforts have been made in philosophy of education to surmount the "is-ought" gap and to draw valid ethical conclusions. Three such efforts will be considered in a search for how (in what sense of an argument, whether in Sense I or Sense II, whether Purist or Capricious) a moral argument is used in philosophy of education, and what difficulties, if any, stand in the way of drawing a valid conclusion in such a moral argument.

The Instrumental Effort

The first of these efforts is the Instrumental, which rests on a means-ends continuum. According to the Instrumental approach, the ends (aims or goals) of education are not isolable from the means (or methods) of education. One must take certain conditions into account if one wishes to achieve an end-in-view. John Dewey writes that "if a person aims to build a bridge, he must build it in a certain way, and of certain materials, or else he will not have a bridge but a heap of stones." [3] Similarly, "given an end, say promotion of health, growth, psychological observations and reflection put us in control of the conditions concerned in that growth." He says, "We know that if we are to get that end, we must do it in a certain way."[4] These means-ends valuations may be expressed in the "if-then" form, e.g., "If you want to be healthy, then take vitamins." One recent Instrumentalist writer points out that if a certain kind of building maximizes learning opportunities for children—which is a desirable end-in-view—then the construction of what kind of school is desirable. The end-in-view considered in the antecedent is "to maximize learning opportunities for children." This remains merely a pious goal, however, until (or unless) it is taken in conjunction with the means necessary to achieve the end-in-view. One of the means (testable empirically) may be the construction of a school building in a certain way, with proper lighting, so many floors, etc.

An evaluative decision, such as the desirability of putting up a new school building in a certain way, is justified by appealing to the antecedent desirability of maximizing learning. Thus, in the words of L. G. Thomas:

> Propositions of this (evaluative) type imply a conditional clause or the interest to be promoted: "You should do this, if you want that outcome." Or to use the "if-then" form of implication, "if I want this interest fulfilled, then I ought to do such and such."[5]

What is "worth having" becomes "the content of the conditional 'if' clause." Thus, according to the Instrumental approach, "if you want to maximize learning experiences, then [you must] construct a school building in a certain way."[6]

But how are we to judge or test whether the desirability characterization or end-in-view is good? To say, "It is desirable to increase learning opportunities" (just as with "It is desirable to prevent or minimize automobile accidents") is to make a value judgment that is not empirically verifiable.[7] Determining the desirability of a goal is not quite the same thing as wanting or prizing it.[8] If there were not this difference, it would be self-contradictory to say, "X is prized" (held dear or wanted; "represents the consummatory focal point of a number of associated interests") on grounds A and B (where A and B are "empirically ascertainable means"), but "still X ought not to be done." That would surely be one instance of not noting the difference between "is" and "ought."

Moreover, the end-in-view or desirability characterization may be incompletely delimited and so encompass value enough to subsume incompatible commands under it. For example, should we increase "opportunities to learn" the evolutionary account of the origin of life on earth? Shall we "increase opportunities to learn" how to annihilate others? Some despicable regime might build schools to increase the learning opportunities for the young to become even more "despicable." And if that example were ruled out as not representing "consummatory focal points of a number of associated interests," one could ask what makes this goal despicable and some other aim praiseworthy? Is it not a persuasive identification of values or interests?

The vagueness of the end-in-view and the resulting incompatibility of opposing ends-in-view (or desirability characterizations) open wide the question "Learning to what end?" Only by a persuasive definition of the phrase "increase learning opportunities" to mean "learn X," together with a previously affirmed *desideratum* of values that people prize, can X be chosen over Y. The "is-ought" gap consequently remains, and while the answer to the question of how to choose an end-in-view may satisfy one sense of an argument, it does not satisfy the one intended.

The Consensual Effort

Another recent effort to draw a satisfactory or justifiable conclusion to a moral argument in education is the Consensual. The "is-ought" distinction is made; judgments of fact are recognized as different from practical (evaluative) judgments; statements in the indicative mood are not considered to be sufficient to imply practical judgments. An attempt is nevertheless made to deal with the difficulty that has stranded the Instrumental effort. What is special about the Consensual effort is the attempt to answer the question of the justification of ends, i.e., how to choose rationally among ends without ignoring the "is-ought" distinction.

The Consensual effort is illustrated in the work of R. Bruce Raup and his associates. They contend that "practical judgments . . . respond to . . . questions in which there is implication of moral responsibility—these questions can readily be given form around the word 'should.' "[9]

To argue for an imperative conclusion in philosophy of education, Raup and his associates have developed what they call the method of "practical intelligence" as a "criterion of community persuasion" for deciding among competing ends-in-view. The notion of "warranted assertibility" proposed in the Instrumental model to conclude a moral argument does not, according to Raup, sufficiently justify a decision on what *should* be done. The criterion of Community Persuasion, which has been carefully spelled out in the writings of Raup, was designed to fill the gap left by the Instrumental effort and to provide a criterion for arriving at some warrantable desirability characterization. Applied to education, this criterion is used to justify a moral decision based on a democratic and uncoerced social consensus.

Raup's Consensual effort has influenced other philosophers of education as well as the social psychologists and guidance personnel of various human-relations groups who are not entirely satisfied with the Instrumental (or scientific) method of drawing moral conclusions. They also prefer not to appeal directly to metaphysical sanctions to justify moral judgments in education. Two versions of the Consensual effort will be considered, to show how it is used. One calls for a reconstructed society, the other for a revival of a nearly authentic religious tradition; both are intended to support moral conclusions in philosophy of education.

According to the Social Reconstructionist version of the Consensual effort, a criterion for choosing among conflicting desirability characterizations[10] is called "the principle of defensible partiality." [11] According to this principle, some ideals among others are worth defending; majority rule decides which they are when unanimity is unobtainable. The paradigm of trial by jury is suggested as a court of final appeal in deciding difficult cases.[12]

If all of mankind thought that X (say, capital punishment) was good, would that make it so? Nose-counting, indicating what *is,* does not imply what *ought to be.* The Consensualist might answer that consensus is not to be taken as extension but intension of the meaning of a moral community. In that sense, it is not self-contradictory to say, "X is *believed by consensus* to be right, even though it is wrong." But to define X persuasively as morally right under these circumstances amounts to ignoring the difference between "is" and "ought."

The nearly religious version of the Consensual effort criticizes and sets out to supplement the Instrumental approach, according to one writer, I. B. Berkson, as follows:

> These many differences between . . . science and ethics . . . disqualify the experimentalist method as a means of establishing the principles of conduct. But there is even a deeper difficulty. In . . . science, objective evidence is possible. In ethics, we can only refer to the opinions of other men. In science, we can have the impersonal evidence of an experimental *test*. In morals, we can only have testimony, the testimony of men of vision, of the poets, the saints, and the philosophers, of men whose lives and whose words evoke a response in us.[13]

It may make for good literary cadence to say that science depends on impersonal tests, whereas ethics depends on the testimony of men. But it makes for rather questionable logic. A testimony is not another kind of test. Hume long ago observed, in his argument on miracles:

> Is the consequence just, because some human testimony has the utmost force and authority in some cases, when it relates the battle of Philippi or Pharsalia, for instance, that therefore all kinds of testimony must in all cases have equal force and authority? [14]

Even if testimony, as distinct from scientific tests, were relevant to morals, testimony that Lincoln was a great moral man might outweigh testimony on the moral greatness of Giordano Bruno or Mahatma Gandhi, or it might be the reverse; yet the weight and degree of testimony for or against a person do not necessarly imply—unless the "is-ought" distinction is waived—moral greatness. And if Berkson means only the testimony of wise or good men or "men of vision," then his argument is circular and begs the question of whether the testimony of men *ought to be a basis for justifying moral judgments.*

Even if testimony were admissible as factual evidence of the values by which people *prefer* to live, such testimony would not furnish a *test* of the values by which people *ought* to live. The Social Reconstructionist version of the Consensual effort hangs by the same limb, whether it is the testimony of those who came before or trial by jury of one's peers (the consensus of others). Even though testimony may persuasively define "what is morally right," that is not sufficient to establish any conclusion as to what people *ought* to believe or by what values they *should* live. For it is possible to say, without self-contradiction: "X is believed by consensus to be right, although it is wrong." To appeal to the Consensual criterion, therefore, is to put forward a moral argument that is persuasive rather than cogently demonstrable.

The A Priori Effort

A third effort to use a moral judgment in philosophy of education is the a priori approach. The logic is intended to be impeccable. A moral conclusion is intended to be true and to follow validly from the premises. The a priori effort, like the deontological (or Intuitionist) ethical viewpoint, emphasizes the cognitive character of ethical statements. Three different versions of the a priori approach will be considered.

The first of these versions is illustrated by the contention of F. J. Sheed, a noted Catholic layman, that we cannot educate children without first knowing "the purpose of life" and that this knowledge can come only from "the revealed word of God." Hence, in the words of one writer, Sheed "has a certain and authoritative answer to the first problem in education, that is, the ends and purposes it should seek to serve." [15]

The following syllogism is designed to show how this conclusion would follow from its premises:

> The purpose of life and education is revealed by the word of God.
>
> One ought to believe in the revealed word of God.
>
> ---
>
> Therefore, one ought to believe in the purpose of life and education as revealed by God.

In seeking to draw a valid and correct ethical conclusion, one begins by assuming the truth of the premises. The first premise states that the purpose of life and education is revealed by the word of God—an affirmation that has not been proved or demonstrated in the philosophically conclusive sense in which it is intended to be taken. One always has to begin with this "if": that the major premise is what one believes. The difficulty is that one may not always believe it. Hence one could always mount an opposing syllogism with the negation of the original major premise and conclude with the contradictory of the previous syllogism—and there would be no way to choose between them.

A second version of the a priori effort to use a moral argument in philosophy of education is illustrated by the following syllogistic reasoning from Mortimer Adler:

> Good habits (virtues) are the same for all men.
>
> Education should aim at the formation of good habits.
>
> ---

> Therefore, education should aim at the same objectives for all men.[16]

One feature of the impeccable logic here is seen in the observance of Hare's principle:

> No imperative conclusion can be validly drawn from a set of premises which does not contain at least one imperative.[17]

The difficulty with this version of the a priori approach, however, is seen when one applies Hare's discussion of descriptive characteristics to the foregoing syllogism. Hare distinguished between the evaluative meaning of a word and the "criteria of application." The evaluative meaning remains the same, but the criteria of application to various contexts may differ. (Toulmin's uses of argument suggest a similar view: see Chapter I.) A good sports car is not the same as a good tennis racket or a good executioner or a good man. These can all be called "good" because the general description of each makes use of evaluative meaning. The descriptive characteristics, however, provide criteria of application and furnish the answer to the follow-up question: "*What* is good about it?"

In connection with the above syllogism, for example, one descriptive question would ask: Education should aim at the formation of what "good habits (virtues)"? (Increasing acuteness of description entails increasing specificity.)

Let us consider loyalty as an example of a "good habit." Substituting "loyalty" for "good habits," we have the following syllogism:

> Loyalty is the same for all men.
>
> Education should aim at the formation of what is the same for all men.
>
> ---
>
> Therefore, education should aim at the formation of loyalty for all men.

To keep the moral characteristic from lacking application, however, the further question arises: Loyalty to whom? Insertion of an additional descriptive characteristic may give rise to the following awkward conclusion:

> Loyalty (to the U.S.S.R.) is the same for all men.
>
> Education should aim at the formation of what is the same for all men.
>
> ---
>
> Therefore, education should aim at the formation of loyalty to the U.S.S.R. for all men.

The difficulty with this version of the a priori approach is that although Adler's more general syllogism follows an impeccable logic, one can aways make new versions by applying descriptive characteristics to it and mount an opposing syllogism next to each new version. One could just as easily substitute U.S. for U.S.S.R. in order to draw a conclusion incompatible with that of the previous syllogism. Arguments that exhibit an impeccable logic, but lack relevance to practical problems, have no use.[18]

The difficulty with the a priori approach (as noted thus far) is that it is either too abstract to have practical application or, once abstractions are replaced by specifics, conclusions follow, if at all, awkwardly, even anomalously. One can, by merely substituting the negation of the major premise, mount an opposing—and equally valid—syllogism next to the original. It is not self-contradictory to deny either the original or the opposing syllogism. Therefore, to define either of these as moral is once again to fail to take note of the difference between "is" and "ought."

In another version of the a priori approach (different in most respects from the foregoing), J. E. McClellan tries to show that "if one is in doubt about the truth of a moral sentence" such as Q, "The use of mechanical contraception is morally wrong," one can "seek evidence concerning the consequences "by a moral truth" like P, "One ought to treat human beings humanely and justly," about which one "is not in doubt." [19] P is analytically true in the sense that "ought" means "treating human beings humanely and justly," and it is thus self-contradictory to say $\sim$ P, "One ought to treat human beings inhumanely and unjustly." The reason for this is that "ought" refers precisely to the sorts of acts that are humane and just; otherwise, "ought" would not have acquired the moral meaning it has.

But, as Moore has shown about defining "good," if P is true by definition, someone else can redefine P so that it is no longer true. (See Chapter II on educational definitions.) Declaring P true on grounds that "ought" means "doing what is humane and just" can be denied by redefining "ought" as "doing one's duty" (like pulling the switch on the electric chair), regardless of whether "it is humane and just." Hence P *can* be denied without self-contradiction, and saying that P is by definition logically undeniable is not noting the difference between "is" and "ought" in the precise fashion called for by Moore.

McClellan, well aware of the "open-question" argument, does not say that P is, strictly speaking, true by definition. Therefore, pressing the "open-question" argument upon P may not be enough. He nevertheless does want P to do the job of a moral truth that is not in doubt and that can help him to judge moral statements such as Q, about which he is in doubt.

There remains the problem of the minor premise. Since the conclusion is Q, the minor is, let us say, $\sim R$, "Not using mechanical contraception is a way of treating human beings humanely and justly." The practical syllogism, then, looks like this (changing only the original Q to read $\sim Q$, and vice versa, for notational convenience):

P_1 One ought to treat human beings humanely and justly.

$\sim R_1$ Not using mechanical contraception is a way of treating human beings humanely and justly.

$\sim Q_1$ Therefore, one ought not to use mechanical contraception ("ought" here means the same thing as morally wrong).

But what happens if, instead, one were to use R_1 to imply Q, as follows:

P One ought to treat human beings humanely and justly.

R_1 Using mechanical contraception is a way of treating human beings humanely and justly.

Q Therefore, one ought to use mechanical contraception.

Granting the moral truth of P, how would this help one to choose between R and $\sim R$, in order to imply either Q or

$\sim Q$? What has happened is that "treating human beings humanely and justly" is identified persuasively by believers of $\sim R$ as not using mechanical contraception, whereas "treating human beings humanely and justly" is identified persuasively by believers of R as using mechanical contraception. The difficulty has been relayed, as with some other a priori arguments involving the minor, but leaving the major anlaytically intact. With which ought the phrase "treating human beings humanely and justly" be identified, "using" or "not using" mechanical contraception? (For this conflict over usage, see also Chapter II on educational definitions.) P is itself necessary, but when it is joined with either R or $\sim R$ (each of which is a persuasive definition), it becomes insufficient to justify either Q or $\sim Q$ as an answer to the moral question "Ought one to use mechanical contraception?"

If we apply this use of argument to education, the same difficulty occurs. Using P as the major, the minor and conclusion are as follows:

P One ought to treat human beings humanely and justly.

R_2 Segregated schooling is a way to treat human beings humanely and justly.

Q_2 Therefore, one ought to favor segregated schooling.

Substitute $\sim R_2$ (in place of R_2); now the conclusion $\sim Q_2$ follows:

P One ought to treat human beings humanely and justly.

$\sim R_2$ Segregated schooling is not a way to treat human beings humanely and justly.

$\sim Q_2$ Therefore, one ought not to favor segregated schooling.

How to choose between Q_2 and $\sim Q_2$?

Or consider:

P_3 One should teach children to treat human beings humanely and justly.

R_3 Respecting private property rights is a way to treat human beings humanely and justly.

Q_3 Therefore, one ought to teach children respect for private property rights.

But, in some other country, using P_3 with $\sim R_3$, "revolutionizing against private property rights" implies $\sim Q_3$ as follows:

P_3 One should teach children to treat human beings humanely and justly.

$\sim R_3$ Revolutionizing against private property rights is a way to treat human beings humanely and justly.

$\sim Q_3$ Therefore, one ought to teach children to revolutionize against private property rights.

Again, how is one to choose between Q_3 and $\sim Q_3$ on the basis of impeccable logic (observance of Hare's rule), given that each has the same true moral premise?

In either case, a wedge R (or $\sim R$) is inserted between P and Q, in order to answer the question of *what sorts of acts* ought to count as humane and just; and this insertion is in the nature of a persuasive definition. (See Chapter II.)

Notice, finally, how this compares with Frankena's analysis of the syllogism:

a. Pleasure is sought by all men.

b. What is sought by all men is good.

---

c. Therefore, pleasure is good.[20]

In this argument, step *b*, just like R (note the analogy), commits the "naturalistic" (or more precisely the "definist") fallacy of using a *persuasive definition* to imply *c* or Q.

The difficulties with the a priori approach, then, are that the major premise can be easily replaced by its negation, resulting in a denial of the original conclusion, and that the minor premise is a persuasive definition. One may accordingly use a moral syllogism to "imply" practical educational conclusions—but only to suit one's own ends. Thus the a priori effort approaches a moral argument in philosophy of education more in the manner of Sense I than in that of Sense II.

Moral as well as metaphysical beliefs are used to imply conclusions to arguments in philosophy of education. The effort to use a moral argument encounters the "is-ought" obstacle—that an ethical conclusion of what ought to be cannot validly be deduced solely from what is. If "is" implied or meant the same thing as "ought," it would be tautological to say, "What is, is right," and self-contradictory to say, "What is, is wrong." The identification of "is" with "ought" would consequently rule out the possibliity of denying (or morally disapproving of) an existing state of affairs, on the grounds that to deny what is, is self-contradictory.[21]

Surmounting the "is-ought" difficulty by validly deducing an ethical conclusion is necessary, though not sufficient, to justify a moral argument in education satisfying Sense II of the word "argument." If "is" meant "ought," one could say: "Killing Jews is done. Therefore, killing Jews is right. This man is a Jew. Therefore, killing him is right." This will not do as a moral conclusion in Sense II, about which one cannot then raise the open question.

Several efforts have been made to use a moral argument in the philosophy of education, taking note of the difference between "is" and "ought" and seeking to draw valid and justifiable conclusions to moral arguments. In the first of these efforts, a consequent end-in-view remains untested by verification of the means without verification of a given end-in-view. In the second, while it is not self-contradictory to say that "X is believed by consensus to be right, although it is wrong," the attempt persuasively to identify consensus with "moral" is an instance of overlooking the difference between "is" and "ought." In the a priori effort, the argument using P to justify Q falls apart if insertion of a different persuasive definition, R or $\sim$R, implies a different conclusion. (Moreover, although, for the most part, it has been assumed with McClellan that P is true, suppose that P_4, "A race of people, by submitting to a thumbscrew from one another, attained to eternal bliss and justice," were true; would that not wreck P?) The difficulty of drawing a conclusion to a moral argument in philosophy of education has not therefore been satisfactorily surmounted by either the Instrumental, the Consensual, or the a priori effort.

On the basis of these observations, a moral argument is used as was the metaphysical argument—not in the sense of an "argument" that is rationally defensible. The attempt has been made to show a difficulty that may have been unrecognized, when moral arguments were used in each of three principal efforts in the philosophy of education.[22] In these efforts, a basis for misgiving occurs, as it did with the metaphysical argument, when the "intentional" use of the word "argument" shifts into the "success" use. There is nothing, however, that is foolish about any of these efforts to draw a defensible conclusion to a moral argument, so long as one does not mistake one sense of "argument" for another. The attempt has not been made to show whether a moral argument can be used but instead to show, in each instance, *how* a moral argument is used. It has been shown that a moral argument is used more like Sense I, even though it is intended to be used in Sense II (that is, in a rationally defensible way).

Noting *how* a moral argument is used may serve as a reminder of the difficulty that results from foregoing the use of an argument in Sense II. Moral arguments are surely not all of the "peach pie" kind (noted in Chapter I, which can be used whimsically—that is, in whichever way one feels like using them). Yet the effort to satisfy Sense II comes up against the "is-ought" hurdle, which has not, in any of the instances noted, been surmounted.

What now? Are we at the end of the road? Are metaphysical and moral arguments in education used in only this way? Shall we rest content with using a moral argument (or a metaphysical argument) with no way to judge one argument as against another? Does not the absence of a conclusion in Sense II (to a metaphysical or moral argument) warrant a counsel of despair? Is it any wonder that one is apt to hear the Emotivist contention that there is really no sense in asking what is right or wrong, since moral valuations are neither true nor false?[23]

1. See Paul F. Schmidt, "Some Criticism of Cultural Relativism," *Journal of Philosophy,* LII (December, 1955), 783.

2. The converse, however, does not hold. A validly deduced conclusion to a moral argument is not thereby shown to be a satisfactory moral decision (nor therefore more like P than C). One might, for example, use the premises: "You ought to kill all these Jews" and "Here is one of them" to deduce validly, "Therefore, you ought to kill him." This "ought" statement is not a satisfactory conclusion to a moral argument for other reasons, which follow subsequently.

3. "The Relation of Theory to Practice in the Education of Teachers," *The Third Yearbook,* National Society for the Scientific Study of Education, Part I (Chicago: University of Chicago, 1904), p. 20.

4. *Ibid.*

5. "Prospects of Scientific Research into Values," *Educational Theory,* VI (October, 1956), 203.

6. *Ibid.*

7. For a related view, see B. Othanel Smith, "A Further Comment on Prospects of Scientific Research into Values," *Educational Theory,* VI (October 1956), 212. In view of Smith's pointed distinction between description and evaluation based on the Emotivist contention, it is surprising to see again, for example, the recent attempt by R. Sleeper to apply science to the problems of ethics in a "scientific ethics." Ralph W. Sleeper, "Non-cognitive Ethics May Not Be What It Seems: A Rejoinder," *Studies in Philosophy and Education,* III (Spring, 1964), 200–201.

8. On this Thomas quotes Dewey: "Valuations exist and are capable of empirical observation, so that propositions about them are empirically verifiable. What individuals and groups hold dear or prize, and the grounds upon which they prize them, are capable in principle of ascertainment, no matter how great the practical difficulties in the way." John Dewey, "Theory of Valuation," *International Encyclopedia of Unified Science,* II (Chicago: University of Chicago, 1939), 58. Dewey, however, distinguished between prizing and appraising. This critique is not intended so much as a critique of Dewey as of Instrumentalism represented here, for example, by Thomas.

9. *The Improvement of Practical Intelligence* (New York: Harper & Bros., 1950), p. 83. The same remark made in criticism of the sort of Instrumentalism exhibited by Thomas is intended to apply also to the Consensual effort expressed here by Brameld. The critique presented here is intended as a criticism of the Consensual effort repre-

sented by Brameld and Berkson rather than of Raup's own conception, which is intended (by the latter) as a "community of persuasion." (I am indebted to Professor Ward Madden for suggesting to me this note of caution in presenting this part of the argument.)

10. This term was first used, I believe, by G. E. M. Anscombe, *Intention* (London: Blackwell, 1957).

11. See Theodore Brameld, *Toward a Reconstructed Philosophy of Education* (New York: Dryden Press, 1956), pp. 200–209.

12. It is known that in a court of law one obtains a verdict by one's peers, but not necessarily the truth, nor even the right verdict. I am indebted for this observation to a friend, Profesor Alfred M. Rifkin.

13. Isaac B. Berkson, *The Ideal and the Community* (New York: Harper & Bros., 1958) p. 59.

14. *An Inquiry Concerning Human Understanding* (New York: The Library of Liberal Arts, 1957), p. 134.

15. See B. Othanel Smith, William O. Stanley, and J. Harland Shores, *Fundamentals of Curriculum Development,* (rev. ed.; Yonkers-on-Hudson, N.Y.: World Book Co., 1957), pp. 531–32.

16. "In Defense of the Philosophy of Education," *Forty-first Yearbook,* National Society for the Study of Education (Chicago: University of Chicago, 1942), p. 239.

17. Richard M. Hare, *The Language of Morals* (London: Clarendon Press, 1952), p. 28.

18. A similar type of syllogism is furnished by Hutchins (see Chapter I), also for the Purist use of argument.

19. "Two Questions about the Teaching of Values," *Educational Theory,* XI (January, 1961), 12.

20. William K. Frankena, "The Naturalistic Fallacy," in Wilfrid Sellars and John Hospers (eds.), *Readings in Ethical Theory* (New York: Appleton-Century-Crofts, 1952), p. 107.

21. This could and even does, it could be argued, daily apply with cruel force in the continuation of educational programs and policies that cannot, even under the most charitable circumstances, count as "educational." Witness woefully inadequate and often harmful schools for the under-privileged.

22. Although the difference between "is" and "ought" is now well enough known to bear repetition, quarrying moral arguments as here done reveals, it seems, an almost inescapable Heisenberg-like

effect in a blending of the one with the other; it may even reach into the field of education where, for example, the idea local people have of an education for good citizenship seems somehow to imply for them a good education, or the idea a philosophical group has either of a good Christian or of a technically well-trained person again somehow seems to imply being "well-educated," as if either of these spelled crowning success in education. It may be that because ongoing education is yet a luxury most of the world over, a little bit of it is thought to be a good thing, which it surely often is; but to this is added the thought that *the education given* is a final good, as well as good through and through, which invariably it never really is.

23. See, for example, Alfred Jules Ayer, *Language, Truth, and Logic* (New York: Dover, 1950), p. 108.

Afterword to Part I and Foreword to Part II

In philosophy of education it is easier to say what arguments are unsatisfactory and why than it is to designate what arguments are satisfactory and how one is to judge among them. Several educational arguments have been analyzed in Part One, and the difficulties of drawing conclusions in this area have been observed. In the two types of metaphysical arguments that involve educational definitions and beliefs, several logical difficulties were noted, such as attempting to conclude with more than was in the premises or drawing an imperative conclusion from descriptive premises. It was pointed out that these difficulties exist whether one uses the constructive or the derivative approach or disclaims both approaches. Three types of moral arguments were found wanting for having more in the conclusion ("ought") than in the premises ("is") or for having empty premises, even though the logic of the argument was impeccable (Hare's rule; see Chapter III).

Thus the impasse discussed in Chapter I was illustrated in Chapters II and III. Evaluative arguments issuing in forms of "Do X" or "Teach X" seemed uniformly to break down. The dilemma appeared to be this: either we adopt the Purist but essentially irrelevant criteria, or we get along with no criteria at all and consequently with no way to judge educational arguments.

Several uses of metaphysical and moral arguments were criticized in Part One on grounds that they "settled" questions in one sense, perhaps, but not in another and far more significant sense. The criticism was more prophylactic than therapeutic: it warned of which arguments to avoid and why; it did not positively propose rational canons of criticism for use in judging which arguments to admit and which to rebut.

The account in Part I of metaphysical and moral arguments in education might compel us to conclude that we have no way out of the Purist-Capricious impasse. Does this mean defeat? Have we no criterion by which to judge what qualifies as a demonstrable argument because we have no true premise from which to infer the truth of the conclusion? Is the Purist ideal only a mathematical logician's dream, empty and impossible in its application to educational arguments?

To counter the thought of surrender in the first round, let it be remembered here that the Purist use of the word "argument," as approximated by formal logic and science, provides a desirable example of univocity and a model of a satisfactory argument. Contrary to Toulmin's appraisal, the historical development of the formal model over the centuries has been a great feat.

Logic and science do not, however, give us the criterion by which to determine which educational arguments we should heed and which we should ignore. The formal requirements of argument are too stringent; the Purist use of argument eliminates educational arguments that we ought not to ignore. On the other hand, the Capricious use admits arguments indiscriminately.

The difficulties of assessing educational arguments were presented in Part I, on the assumption that knowledge of what is wrong precedes discovery of what may be right.

An attempt to test the mettle of educational arguments with rational canons of criticism will be made in Part Two. This attempt will include an indication of the scope and limits of reason through an assessment of metaphysical and moral arguments in education in a way that is intended to avoid the Purist-Capricious dilemma and to move, somewhat, toward justifying Sense II of the word "argument."

It may be anticipated that there is indeed a way out of the impasse—small, but sufficient to give some rational basis for judging educational arguments. The problem—even if the forthcoming solution is wrong—consists in discerning some characteristics or canons of criticism X or Y that give us a rational basis for judging which arguments to admit and which to eliminate or rebut.

The solution will suggest a third use of argument as a way out of the impasse. There may be a use of argument that is not so restrictive as to exclude all educational arguments and yet not so open as to admit all such arguments indiscriminately. Some have the idea that the question "Why should the humanities be taught?" requires an *argument* for its answer—a set of premises fitted to an assumed logical model so that they constitute good reasons for assenting to "The humanities should be taught." [1] That idea is tied neither to the Purist mathematical logician's model nor to the Capricious use of argument such as we have found in some "answers" offered by philosophers of education to educational questions. Relative to the possible third use of argument (which is not like Sense I or Sense II), Israel Scheffler writes:

> We do not consider it a matter of indifference or whim just what the educator chooses to teach. Some selections we judge better than others; others we deem positively intolerable. Nor are we content to discuss . . . issues

of selection as if they hinged on personal taste alone. We try to convince others; we present *ordered arguments;* we appeal to relevant consequences and implicit commitments.[2]

On what grounds do we judge some decisions to be better than others? Our third use will not be shown to resemble Sense II; but it need not, for that reason, be capricious. (This will need proving in future chapters.) Our third use of argument suggests a way out of the Purist-Capricious dilemma. Although not identical with either the use of argument in mathematical logic or with Sense I arguments, this use of argument may resemble the kind of philosophical arguments for which Frederick Waismann pleads,[3] and which Ryle cites as the philosopher's tool in trade. It may resemble the philosophical use of the *reductio ad absurdum,*[4] which Toulmin and Hare and other (analytic) philosophers examplify in ethics,[5] and which, according to one dictionary definition, means "to offer reasons for or against something." [6]

Whether we can discover reasons that will satisfy something like Sense II (while still not Purist) has now to be considered.

1. See McClellan, "Why Should the Humanities Be Taught?"

2. "Justifying Curricular Decisions."

3. "How I See Philosophy," in Alfred Jules Ayer (ed.), *Logical Positivism* (Glenncoe, Ill.: Free Press, 1959).

4. G. Ryle, "Philosophical Arguments," in Ayer (ed.), *Logical Positivism.*

5. Stephen Edelston Toulmin, *An Examination of the Place of Reason in Ethics* (Cambridge: Cambridge University Press, 1950).

6. *Webster's Collegiate Dictionary* (Springfield, Mass.: G. & C. Merriam Co., 1953), p. 57.

Part II. The Place of Reason in Assessing Educational Arguments

IV. *The Place of Metaphysical Reasons in Education*

The view that the metaphysical approach encourages philosophers of education to perpetrate "garrulous absurdities" has recently been voiced more gently than it was by Sidney Hook. Sterling McMurrin maintains that metaphysics is, in principle, irrelevant to education and that it is a mistake to think educational theories "can and should be derived from metaphysical premises." [1] This contention (despite some slight modification of the "absurdity" idea) may be dubbed the "hard-line," "tough-minded," or Purist approach, for it is analogous to the Purist use of argument that we have noted. If it is correct, it means elimination *in toto* of any relation between metaphysics and education.

Opposed, of course, to the "hard-line" or "tough-minded" approach is what, after the fashion distinguished by William James, may be called the "soft-line" or "tender-minded" approach, which consists in drawing educational conclusions from metaphysical beliefs. One difficulty with the use of the hard-line seems to be its comparison of educational arguments with arguments in mathematics or science. Its consequent exclusion of metaphysics from educational arguments is described by at least one writer as an effort to throw the baby out with the bath.[2] The tough-minded or hard-line approach, like the Purist use of argument, which refuses to admit all metaphysical and evaluative arguments, excludes too much.

Frankena's MEM premises

One proposed solution is Frankena's contention that some metaphysical premises are relevant and necessary, although not sufficient for implying and justifying educational conclusions, and that consequently not all metaphysical arguments are mistaken in principle. He uses a device that he calls MEM's, his abbreviation for metaphysical, epistemological, and meta-ethical premises. Taken "together with other true or acceptable (factual or valuational) premises," MEM's, according to Frankena, could even be said to be sufficient to justify some educational conclusions.

In suggesting how this might be so, Frankena seems to have suggested a way to loosen the vise that has clamped philosophy of education between the jaws of Positivism and traditional metaphysics. Surely if an argument had premises that would both imply and be sufficient to justify an educational conclusion, it would provide the basis for judging educational arguments. We could then show that one argument is justified, while another is not. If that could be shown, we would be able to judge educational arguments without "throwing the baby out with the bath." If Frankena could establish which MEM's are necessary, we could use these together with other necessary premises, moral, factual, pedagogical, etc., to arrive at a basis for judging educational arguments. And we could do this without either admitting or banishing all metaphysics indiscriminately, by fiat or by persuasive definition.

It will be useful to examine briefly what Frankena says with regard to the use of MEM's for implying and justifying educational conclusions.

Frankena tries to show that derivation of educational theory from metaphysics is not necessarily mistaken in principle; he claims that those like Sterling McMurrin, who contend that the derivation from metaphysics to education is mistaken or "obstinate" or "futile," have failed to establish their position.[4]

He concedes that some MEM's seem to have little if anything to do with the aims and methods of education. For instance:

1. All that exists is mental or spiritual.
2. The object known is not dependent on its being known for its existence or its properties.
3. There are universals, abstract particulars, etc.
4. Intrinsic goodness is a simple, non-natural quality.

But other MEM premises may have some logical connection with theories of education. For instance:

5. Some of our knowledge is innate.
6. There is a God.
7. We have immortal souls and what we believe and do in this life makes a difference in what we shall experience in the next.[5]

Even though the metaphysical premise may not be sufficient, Frankena says that "it does not follow that the metaphysical premise is not relevant or even that it is not necessary. All that follows is that it is not sufficient by itself." [6] He offers one example:

> Consider the theistic belief that there is a God defined in the traditional Judeo-Christian way. I too doubt that, taken just by itself, it can be said logically to entail any conclusions about how or what to teach or why to teach it, but I find it hard to believe that it is logically irrelevant to such conclusions if it is taken together with other premises either of a factual or ethical kind. For example, if we add the premise that this God ought to be obeyed or that He is the end of all human striving (and yet others), it does seem to me that it may follow logically that we ought to take obedience to Him or communion with Him as an aim of education (at least in non-public schools).[7]

"More generally," says Frankena,

> I am inclined to agree with McMurrin that MEM premises, taken singly and by themselves, do not suffice to establish any conclusions about the methods and aims of education. It does not follow, however, that they are not necessary to do so, or that they are irrelevant to doing so. It may still be that educational conclusions *cannot be justified without* MEM premises, and it may also still be that, taken together with certain other true or acceptable premises (factual or valuational), MEM premises *suffice to justify such conclusions.*[8]

Accordingly,

> . . . MEM premises by themselves probably do not suffice logically to establish educational conclusions . . . , but it does seem to me that at least some of them, if true, are relevant to such conclusions. . . .

Moreover,

> . . . Some educational conclusions do presuppose certain MEM premises, e.g., that communion with God is the end or at least one of the ends of education. If we assume that education ought not to seek to promote this end if there is no God, then the belief that it ought to promote this end requires the premise that there is a God for its justification.[9]

A Difficulty with Frankena's Approach

Thus Frankena tries to show that the derivation of educational theory from metaphysics is not necessarily mistaken. One may note how he attempts to avoid the "is-ought" fallacy and to refrain from stating more in the conclusion than there is in the premises. To the metaphysical premise "There is a God," he adds the further statement "God ought to be obeyed," and combines these with a premise concerning obedience as an aim of education, concluding that obedience to God ought to be an aim of education.[10]

Frankena unfortunately involves himself in a difficulty. If he means that philosophy X logically implies educational conclusion Y, then, given his additional MEM premises and factual premises, his conclusion is valid but trivial. If he means that the philosophy of X not merely *logically implies,* but in some other significant sense *implies and justifies,* educational conclusion Y, then, given his additional premises, he arrives at a conclusion that is perhaps interesting but is invalid.

To the educational conclusion that obedience to God should be an aim of education, Frankena adds the parenthetical phrase "at least in non-public schools." When a person associated with an ism and backed by its metaphysical belief says, "I believe in the philosophy of X," and (with all the logically requisite premises to imply *teaching* for aim Y) concludes, "therefore we *ought to* teach Y in our particular schools," the phrase "in our particular schools" is crucial. (Notice its similarity to Frankena's remark in parentheses, "at least in non-public schools.") Remove that phrase and one can infer that we ought to teach X *at large* (precisely what the educational debate is all about). The proposal to teach X is made not merely to teach one's flock but to propagate the faith at large. If Frankena's inclusion of the phrase in parentheses is meant to confine the teaching to theistic schools, then his implication is logical but trivial. Each ism—Lutheranism or Thomism, for example—says that its religious philosophy implies its aims of education for its own followers and their young. The issue, however, is whether to teach X (some religion) at large; and this is not settled by logical implication (for reasons subsequently to be cited). If Frankena intends that obedience to God ought to be an aim of education for schools at large, he seeks to conclude with more than there was in the premises. If he does not intend this, then he has not shown that metaphysics is relevant or necessary to an educational conclusion that applies at large. Frankena, it seems, either establishes his case by trivializing it or fails to establish that MEM's even imply, much less justify educational conclusions, if more is intended than logical implication.[11]

The idea that MEM's, though not sufficient, are necessary to imply and to justify educational conclusions does have an important consequence: An argument that not only implies, but also justifies, one conclusion shows that an incompatible conclusion is *not* justified. It thus provides a basis for judging among educational arguments, so that one can say, "This argument is justified, that one is not." But to justify an educational conclusion, such as teaching obedience to God, requires more than Frankena has in his premises. One could always mount a contrary metaphysical premise, "There is no God," and join that premise with other MEM and factual and valuational premises to deny that we should teach obedience to God. Frankena does not show what is necessary, let alone sufficient, to justify an educational conclusion. To state MEM premises on behalf of teaching obedience to God, with no accompanying argument to show why one cannot mount an opposing argument and draw a contradictory conclusion, does not seem to justify the first argument. What does it mean to "justify" an educational conclusion, if not to put up the reasons why one conclusion is justifiably preferred to the other?

If one were to equate implication with justification, a particular ism could not merely imply, but would also have to justify an educational conclusion; its conclusion would apply not only to one particular school system but to all school systems. The attempt to equate implication with justification could be countered by mounting Moore's "open-question" argument against it. One could argue that to say that X implies Y but does not justify Y is not self-contradictory; hence, the two are not synonymous. While Frankena did not say that implication and justification were synonymous, he shifted by scarcely perceptible steps from "follow logically" to "establish" to "justified"; as Hume said, in a similar connection, this shift "is of the last consequence." It seems incumbent on anyone who claims to imply and to justify a conclusion that he state his case so as to defend his own conclusion, or that he mount his argument against a contradictory conclusion.[12] It is not enough to attempt to draw a logical implication from God's existence to the conclusion that an aim of education is obedience to God. By neglecting the far harder task of justifying his conclusion, Frankena has failed to show, it seems, even the necessity, let alone the sufficiency of some MEM's, along with other premises, to justify educational conclusions.

How—on Frankena's grounds—does one go about testing MEM premises? He speaks of their being "true or acceptable premises," as follows:

> It may still be that educational conclusions cannot be justified without MEM premises, and it may still be that, taken together with certain other true or acceptable premises (factual or valuational), MEM premises suffice to justify such conclusions. . . . MEM premises by themselves probably do not suffice logically to establish educational conclusions . . . , but it does seem to me that at least some of them, if true, are relevant to such conclusions.[13]

Does Frankena mean that *some* MEM's are true? Are some MEM premises true and others acceptable? How does one establish which MEM's are true? What is the test? [14] The truth of some, but not all, of the premises does not imply that the conclusion is true. Only if *all* the premises are true have we any reason to accept the conclusion as true. (See Chapter I on Smullyan's idea of a *sound* argument.) To show that the conclusion is true, Frankena would have to show that the premises are also true, for it is the truth of the premises that implies the truth of the conclusion.

Even when the premises are true, the implication is only that the conclusion is true, not that it is justified. How does one show that, besides being valid and having true premises and a true conclusion, an argument is justified?

While Frankena distinguishes between necessary and sufficient premises in relation to a valid educational conclusion, his analysis of MEM's does not show how to justify one educational conclusion over another. How would one show, for example, that there is a God, or that we ought to have communion with Him?

Frankena refers to premises that are "true or acceptable." But a problem like that with "true" premises may arise with "acceptable" premises. Frankena simply does not show what counts as being acceptable, although it does seem that anyone who tries to make a case for "acceptable" premises would also try to show how he distinguishes between acceptable and unacceptable premises.

Even if we had "acceptable" premises, would that suffice to show that the conclusion was justified? Imagine the following discussion at a principal's conference:

A. A lunch program that meets minimal daily dietary needs, since it is nutritionally adequate, meets the needs and is therefore acceptable.

B. This program certainly does meet *minimum* standards of acceptability, but is the minimum that we as a community can give *justified*?

"Acceptable" means "worthy of acceptance" and also means "minimally passable." Moore rebutted the identification of pleasure with good by pointing out that "X causes pleasure but X is not good" is not self-contradictory; similarly, one can answer, "No," without self-contradiction, to the question "Practice X is acceptable, but is it justified?" [15] While many "acceptable" practices are also "justifiable," these terms are ordinarily used to give a latitude to acceptable but to impose a restriction on "justifiable." "Acceptable" may mean both "worthy of" and "capable of"; not so, "justifiable."

For these reasons, true or acceptable MEM premises seem not to be sufficient, nor are they even shown to be necessary to justify educational conclusions. The statement that MEM's (plus factual and valuational premises) are true or acceptable implies no more than that the educational conclusion drawn from them is true or acceptable; it does not imply that the conclusion is justifiable. Frankena's syllogism relating to religion does not furnish an instance of a necessary premise that justifies an educational conclusion because one can easily mount an opposing syllogism that negates the opening premise and consequently denies the educational conclusion. For example:

> The idea of a Christian God is a false idea or fiction.
> One ought not to teach with obedience or allegiance to a false idea or fiction as an aim of education.
>
> ---
>
> Therefore, one ought not to teach with obedience or allegiance to the idea of a Christian God as an aim of education.

How can one tell which MEM's are true, acceptable, or justifiable? How can one choose between one set of premises

(MEM) and a contradictory set ($\sim$ MEM) in order to justify one educational conclusion over its contradictory. Frankena does not show how one rebuts a MEM or its contradictory; yet this is surely one minimal requirement for being able to speak of justifying an educational conclusion.

A Related Difficulty

Frankena made a comment on Smith regarding the necessity of metaphysics to education. Smith had said:

> Even if a philosophy of education were derivable from a metaphysical position, it would be impossible to build the educational program upon it.[16]

Smith gave two reasons:

> For one thing, if it were necessary first to agree upon a metaphysics before we could agree upon an educational program, we should have to close the schools. For another thing, the factors determining what an educational program shall be are so varied and interrelated that the implications of any particular metaphysics will be lost as the program is shaped.[17]

It is, of course, an empirical proposition whether agreement on a metaphysical view implies the opening or closing of schools. According to Smith's proposition, any metaphysical view can be made to seem compatible with the operation of the schools; no particular metaphysical view is necessary to the schools. But that does not mean that "metaphysics" is not needed; it means only that some given metaphysical view or ism is not required for the operation of the schools. One could argue quite plausibly that a completely satisfactory education cannot wholly exclude reference to all past philosophy, especially the metaphysics of such great philosophers as Plato and Aristotle, etc. Smith gives his own case away when he speaks of "a metaphysical position." No one argues for that any more than anyone insists that governments would have to give up their power unless they could establish it on the foundations of a particular ethical or metaphysical system. Yet it is quite clear, surely, that an ideally satisfactory theory of government would not wholly exclude reference to all past philosophy, the history of ethics or metaphysics. It is equally clear that we do not have to agree on a metaphysical or ethical viewpoint before we can have a functioning police force, a fire department, a tax structure, a highway system, sewage or garbage disposal, and all the rest. Nevertheless, one's philosophical conception of man and society requires reference, however oblique, indirect, or strained, to metaphysics—not to "a metaphysical position" but to metaphysics. Philosophy as well as philosophy of education requires reference to the sort of *metaphysical dialogue* for which Plato, among others, has been so responsible and which makes the ultimate metaphysical questions from Thales to the present perhaps the *most ultimately significant* questions that the mind of man can ask. Frankena's mistake, like Smith's, may lie in having confused "a metaphysics" with "metaphysics."

That mistake may explain why Smith's objections to, and Frankena's defense of, deriving educational conclusions from particular metaphysical doctrines never seem very convincing. They both move (Hume's move "of the last consequence") from the particular to the universal. But when they deny that the conclusion is universal and attempt, instead, to apply a particular conclusion only to a particular school system or to a particular metaphysical doctrine, then they succeed only in restating the obvious (that, as Christians, they are in favor of Christian education for their fellow Christians).

To summarize thus far: Frankena tries to show that MEM's, while not by themselves *sufficient,* are sometimes *relevant to,* and even *necessary for,* drawing educational conclusions. He starts with the position that there is a God and adds to this metaphysical premise the moral premise that God ought to be obeyed. Then he holds that these premises, even though they are not sufficient, are necessary to imply the educational conclusion that obedience to God ought to be an aim of education. The attempt has been made to show that Frankena either trivialized or invalidated his conclusion. It would be trivialization if he intended to confine his educational conclusion to schools of a particular sect (say, Lutherans or Thomists). The charge of circularity might then also be in order, even though this type of logical implication as a test of consistency may play a preliminary sort of role in arguments in educational philosophy. It would be invalidation of the conclusion if, going beyond his conclusion, Frankena recommended that obedience to God should be an aim of education *at large.* In what sense, then, does Frankena say that some MEM's are necessary to imply and to justify some educational conclusions?

His further attempt to show this—if the MEM, factual, or valuational premises are "true" or "acceptable"—does not seem very successful either, partly because Frankena does not successfully pit the MEM's that he cites against a contradictory set of MEM premises that would seem to be a minimal requirement for MEM's to justify an educational conclusion.

Moreover, it has not been shown in what respect the philosophical or valuational premises are "true" or "acceptable."

And even if they were "true" or "acceptable," this would still not mean that they were justifiable.

Finally, as to Smith's argument that if agreement first had to be reached on a metaphysical position, the schools would have to be closed, the attempt has been made to distinguish between a particular and a universal. Of course, in a trivial sense, the schools would not be able to function if their operation had to depend on prior agreement about a metaphysical position, but neither would any aspect of government: a tax structure, a police force, a garbage disposal unit. Agreement on a particular metaphysical position, however, is not identical with agreement that metaphysics is necessary to education; it can be argued that no philosophy of education (nor any completely satisfactory education) can completely exclude metaphysics. In that sense, metaphysics is seen to be necessary to education.

Frankena's analysis rests, as has been indicated, on the mistake of a conclusion that contained more than there was in the premises. This was revealed by his assertion that some MEM premises can be justified on grounds they are implied with true or acceptable premises, although the meaning of neither truth nor acceptability was shown. In proposing a philosophical scheme for justifying some educational conclusions, however, he suggested what might be required. Accordingly, something can be said for his scheme. If, as a result of it, we were able to point even minimally to what would justify an educational conclusion, we might thereby direct ourselves toward judging educational arguments. If some MEM's could justify some educational conclusions by meeting and defeating opposing conclusions, our observation of what justifies some MEM's and does not justify others might afford us a basis for judging one metaphysical argument against another. If, however, it could not be shown how some MEM's are necessary to justify some educational conclusions nor how one can judge between philosophical arguments in education, then this would not be the way out of the Purist-Capricious impasse (and there might be no way out at all).

In sum, Frankena holds that some MEM's are relevant and necessary but not sufficient to imply and justify some educational conclusions. But how does one choose between one set of MEM premises and a contradictory set, ~ MEM? MEM's do not, at least as presented, seem to give us a rational basis for deciding between contradictory educational conclusions of the kind "Teach obedience to God" and "Don't teach that sort of obedience." And so Frankena's attempt turns out to be another effort in behalf of metaphysical argument in education that is an argument only in Sense I, "response," and not in Sense II, "solution."

It has not yet been shown how some metaphysical premises go farther than mere presuasion to imply and justify some educational conclusions in, or as in, Sense II.

Educational Metaphors

To assess a metaphysical premise in an educational argument, one might first see the role of the premise in education. A metaphysical premise in education is sometimes expressed as a metaphor or word picture, delineating the ideal purposes, functions, and interrelations of man, society, and the cosmos. The metaphor or word picture may even be comprehensive enough to include reference to man's ultimate destiny.

If we could find some characteristic or criterion by which to make a critical evaluation of educational metaphors that are expressed as metaphysical premises, we would have a more satisfactory means of appraisal than Frankena's. We could then say that if this characteristic is present in an educational argument, it, rather than its contradictory, would count as a good reason for drawing an educational conclusion.

It may be recalled that Frankena's effort to show the relationship between metaphysics and education through the use of MEM premises did suggest what a justifiable argument would look like. But his detailed scheme of justification showed no known true or acceptable metaphysical premises to help one decide among rival educational conclusions concerning which educational policy ought to be adopted—not only for schools of one denomination but for schools for all. This was the issue in the educational argument, and on this point Frankena clearly did not succeed in showing how MEM's help to justify educational conclusions.

Although there are no known methods of criticism to which metaphysical premises are directly open, the educational metaphor has been used to express various metaphysical views of the cosmos, of God, of man and society. As Othanel Smith has expressed it:

> . . . Any philosophical system will include a picture of man and society. In so far as it deals with man's nature, his development and his destiny, the system will necessarily have implications for the education of man. And these implications when spelled out may be called a philosophy of education.[18]

Scheffler's study of educational metaphors has shown that there are grounds for subjecting metaphors to rational criticism. Some analogies may be trivial and some analogies (as in the case of the child compared to a plant in a garden) have limits, and therefore break down in certain contexts.[19] Scheffler shows that metaphysical premises do not have to be considered exempt from the application of rational canons of criticism.

Thus one way to use rational canons of criticism in assessing metaphysical arguments in education consists in a consideration of metaphorical statements or "root metaphors." In this connection, Frankena did not take note of Smith's comment that "any philosophical system will include a picture of man and society,"[20] nor did he show in any other way what is necessary in order to justify an educational conclusion.

The notion of a picture or metaphor may provide a clue to how some MEM's help to justify some educational conclusions and may give us a basis for judging between one set of MEM premises and another. There may be no rational way to decide between the metaphysical premises "There is a God" and "There is no God." But there may be a way to employ rational canons of criticism so as to choose between one metaphor or picture of the relations of man, society, the cosmos, and God, and a rival metaphor that pictures these relations very differently. If metaphors could be criticized in this way, it might be possible to show how metaphysics is necessary, even if not sufficient, to justify a general educational conclusion or, at any rate, to provide some rational way of evaluating a metaphysical premise in an educational argument. But Frankena did not examine the metaphorical character of metaphysical premises.

A metaphor suggests an analogy, presented in a pictorial and sometimes insightful way, in which something well known may illuminate something less well known. According to Israel Scheffler:

> . . . We may regard the metaphorical statement as indicating that there is an important analogy between two things.[21]

Implicit also in the use of a metaphor is the idea of testing an analogy, a common and legitimate device in philosophy. Scheffler therefore suggests this mode of criticism:

> First, we may reach the conclusion that a given metaphor is trivial or sterile, indicating analogies that are, in context, unimportant. Second, we may determine the limitations of a given metaphor, the points at which the analogies it indicates break down.[22]

Observation of the function of educational metaphors may indicate their bearing on the use of metaphysical premises. It remains to be seen whether examination of metaphors will provide a way of determining which metaphysical arguments to admit and will thus help to resolve the dilemma of rigidity versus looseness in judging metaphysical arguments in education. It will be contended here that an examination of educational metaphors does offer a way, at least partially, to apply rational canons of criticism to metaphysical arguments.

Root Metaphors

Philosophers of education sometimes ask metaphysical questions that do not call for educational definitions or metaphysical concepts of the purposes of education; in place of the question "What is the meaning and purpose of education?", some of them ask, "What is your 'root metaphor' (or social or educational metaphor) of the educated man?"[23]

Such picture-preferences, generally designated in philosophy of education as root metaphors, are meant to describe the ideally educated person. They are also intended to provide a picture of how the individual develops from childhood into adulthood. The child has been pictured as a blank tablet upon which experience is written or as a statue in the making—essentially passive and undynamic; and the child has been pictured as a flower that grows after the teacher has gone—essentially alive and active but with an unspecified aim or direction of growth. The educational metaphor conveys beliefs about the way in which the child develops, about the role of the teacher,[24] about the aims, method, and content of education, and about the role of the school in society. Such a metaphor may refer, in passing, to a view of the cosmos, of the nature and destiny of man (whether naturalistic or supernaturalistic), and to some even more abstract metaphysical categories, such as the one or the many, change or permanence.

When the metaphor has been stated, the next step is to begin to spell out a system of education. This initially takes the form of an educational proposal, designed to provide satisfactory answers to such basic educational questions as what, how, or whom to teach.[25] The curriculum proposal, although not an integral part of the metaphor, is derived from the metaphor as a sort of explication or analysans (a "spelling out") of what the metaphor intended to convey. It is sometimes identified as a deduction or implication of what, how, and whom to teach, based on an explication of the contents of the metaphor. This sort of implication has been called a "formal" or "logical implication" [26] (of the kind noted in Chapter II concerning the derivation of educational conclusions from metaphysical beliefs or isms). The question at this point is whether the proposal is consistent with the metaphor or picture-preference of the educated man that is actually believed and endorsed.[27] Now, it would be inconsistent for Hutchins, whose picture-preference is the classical "cultivation of the intellect," to propose an educational curriculum emphasizing a "life-adjustment" program that would interfere with the study of the Great Books. Since Hutchins did, in fact, propose the teaching of the Great Books rather than "life-adjustment" experiences, his educational proposals may be considered "logically implied in" his belief in the development of the intellect. For a proposal to be "logically implied in" a metaphor or a metaphysical belief—which itself may be suggested by a metaphor—the proposal must be the articulation of what is contained in the metaphor. It must unpack the metaphor, so to speak. An educational philosopher uses a metaphor or a metaphysical belief to imply logically a proposal that he regards as consistent with his belief. Thus a metaphysical belief may allude to an educational philosopher's picture-preference or root metaphor of an ideally educated person, and when this has been fully explicated ("spelled out"), it evolves an educational proposal.

A root metaphor or picture-preference is used to guide—in this sense, "imply"—the scope and sequence of one's desired educational curriculum. In this use of metaphor, we cannot outline the scope of an educational curriculum without revealing our root metaphor or social metaphor. The social metaphor is therefore an indispensable condition for effective curriculum-making. B. Othanel Smith says:

> It is to be noted that educational purposes go back ultimately to social metaphor. Everyone carries around in his head a picture of what society is or ought to be. This picture embraces, in ideal form, the type of individual called for by the society, and the relations envisioned among those individuals.[28]

The metaphor serves also to inspire action in the formulation of educational programs that are designed to carry out the purposes suggested by the metaphor. An educational metaphor does have its deliberative function and exhorts the profession to embrace and implement the picture of man and society that it contains.

These metaphors are often theoretically illuminating and suggest fertile and far-reaching uses of educational language to depict ideal conditions. But when root metaphors are used as sufficient or even necessary conditions of an effective educational program or are presented in a form that is closed to appropriate criticism, they invite misgiving. Whatever may be a metaphor's *theoretically suggestive qualities,* a metaphor has not been shown to be either *a necessary or a sufficient condition* for choosing one curriculum rather than some other,[29] any more than has an expression of educational definition, purpose, or belief. This may explain what those who hold the hard-line approach find objectionable in the purported relation of metaphysics to education.

Philosophers of education can and do give reasons for proposing one curriculum rather than another and one course rather than another; among those reasons, some subject matter may be lighted up by a metaphor—if subjected to appropriate criticism—although an overextended metaphor may obscure more than it illuminates. The luminosity depends on how a metaphor is used. A well-used metaphor may even reveal a key to unlocking aims and areas of education that would otherwise be hidden. But when a metaphor is used in lieu of an argument, shut against appropriate criticism, or when *any single* educational metaphor—alias "purpose of education"—is used as either a sufficient or a necessary condition for determining the contents of the curriculum, serious doubts may arise.

The Residual Problem

According to Smith:

> Educational purposes are rooted in [social metaphors] and the settling of disagreements about these purposes therefore demands agreement about the kind of society people desire. Since consensus about what society ought to be has never been attained, and is not apt to be reached, the question of educational purposes promises to be perennial.[30]

While we agree on a "minimum of knowledge and skills to be taught, aimed at reducing ignorance and incompetence as much as possible," the meaning and purpose of education continue to be debated in terms of a "residual concept." [31]

The residual problem remains of why one ought to choose metaphor X rather than Y. Moving from MEM's to metaphors only moves the problem of deciding between X and Y from one form of expression in education to another. The picturesqueness of the metaphor makes it richer than the MEM but does not inherently support a choice between metaphors X and Y.

Smith says that every educational philosopher has a metaphor in mind; its function is presumably to guide one's choice of what, how, or whom to teach. The difficulty, just as with educational definitions, is this: If we ask, "What is your social metaphor of education?", Hutchins articulates his view of education as the "cultivation of intellectual virtues";

Dewey articulates the ideal of growth; and Kilpatrick expresses his picture-preference that education should seem like "life itself." [32] But when one man puts forward metaphor X, and another advocates metaphor Y, how does one make a choice?

Unfortunately, as Scheffler points out, educational metaphors—unlike physical theories—cannot be judged cumulatively or placed side by side for comparison. He says:

> . . . It seems mistaken to try to find a progressive order of metaphors in education, each metaphor more adequate and comprehensive than the last.[33]

However, other ways of testing an educational metaphor are suggested by Scheffler's two modes of criticism relating to triviality in analogy and to limitation of analogy. These modes of criticism may be applied to the metaphors of the plant, the block of marble, and the blank tablet. The comparison of a child with a plant, a block of marble, or a blank tablet may be evaluated as to basic limitations and fruitfulness of implications. For example, a child is not inanimate like a slab of marble, and thus an initial deficiency appears in the comparison. This mode of criticism uses appeal to factual considerations in evaluating comparisons. In the metaphors examined by Scheffler, facts can be appealed to in order to note any limitation in an expression.

Religious and metaphysical metaphors involving belief or disbelief in God and connected with comprehensive and otherworldly questions are far more difficult to assess because the facts necessary for comparison may not be available. Scheffler's modes of criticism may be applied to these more troublesome sorts of metaphor too. But there are added problems in dealing with metaphors that depict the structure and relations of an ideal society or of the universe at large and that culminate in a theological metaphor concerning whether or not there is a God.

There is a marked difference between the metaphors that Scheffler examined and those that Smith examined. Scheffler's this-worldly, epistemologically-oriented metaphors concern comparisons between a single mind or an individual and some natural process or product, while Smith's other-worldly, metaphysical or root metaphors, of the kind that Stephen C. Pepper introduced into philosophical discussion,[34] concern comparisons between an individual or a single mind and society or the cosmos at large. The use of root metaphors or basic attitudes toward education is not the same kind of thing that Scheffler discusses. Dewey's metaphor of the school as the "embryo of society," for example, or Plato's metaphor of the cave, is far more comprehensive in basic outlook than the plant, clay, or tablet metaphors of the child cited in Scheffler's epistemologically-oriented account. This difference is not necessarily a drawback; it makes it possible to distinguish the down-to-earth metaphors studied by Scheffler from root metaphors, as first discussed by S. C. Pepper, and first discussed in philosophy by B. Othanel Smith

Testing other-worldly root metaphors by factual comparisons is vastly more difficult than testing this-worldly metaphors in this way. The modes of criticism cited by Scheffler call for finding and stating "truths in the phenomena before us." Dewey's growth metaphor is true to the extent that children are in fact alive and growing organisms. By the same criterion, we detect the false aspects of the clay tablet and marble slab metaphors, in that children are not inert matter.

The residual difficulty consists in attempting to choose among conflicting root metaphors—between those of Dewey and Hutchins or between the Thomist or the Marxist root metaphors.

Educational Bliks

"Bliks" are another way of expressing root metaphors.[35] A blik is a basic attitude toward the world, "a habitual and confirmed way of seeing things." Recent philosophical discussions of bliks pinpoint the difficulties facing educationists, who have meager or no modes of criticism by which to judge philosophical arguments in education. Similar difficulties exist for religious discourse, which the notion of bliks was intended to clarify. A consideration to bliks may suggest a way to assess metaphysical premises in education because the philosophical dialogue about bliks is focused on applying rational canons of criticism to troublesome arguments. The notion of educational bliks is extended here with the intention of projecting an enlarged picture of the problem that we face in evaluating metaphysical arguments in education.

A way to choose among metaphysical and theological arguments has been suggested by R. M. Hare's (and others') discussions of the blik notion. Hare and others—although they differ about how to do it—attempt to tell the difference between a *right* and a *wrong* blik.[36] If the method of distinguishing between a right and a wrong blik could be incorporated in the criticism of metaphysical premises, it might provide a basis for deciding between a MEM and its contradictory, ~ MEM. In other words, if some process could show an educational blik, which is comparable with an educational metaphor, to be right or wrong, that same process could also be used to judge metaphysical premises in educational arguments.

The notion of educational bliks is not intended to be wholly, or even largely, separated from that of educational metaphors. There are, of course, differences. A metaphor is intended to evoke a picture for comparison with some actual or ideal state of affairs. A blik is one's total attitude, but that does not preclude its being expressed in pictorial analogies; in fact, most of the recent discussions of bliks contain parables that evoke pictorial images for comparison with real or imagined or ideal states of affairs. There is, we might say, "a family resemblance" between metaphors and bliks.

It is contended here that a distinction between a right blik and a wrong blik can be made, can be applied to an educational metaphor that is used as a metaphysical premise, and thus can be used to evaluate a metaphysical premise in education.

Hare parallels the distinction between a right and a wrong blik with a difference between a sane and an insane blik. He cites as an example of an insane blik the case of a graduate student at Oxford who thinks the professors are "out to get him," although they show the greatest kindness and concern for him. Hare cites his own trust that the steel of his car will not fall apart—a right belief, in Humean terms, that enables him to continue to drive—as an example of a *sane* blik. Hare conjectures that if he acquired the fear that his car would disintegrate for no reason—and regardless of demonstrations of safety, he refused to enter the car—he would have an insane blik, out of kilter with reality, *wrong*. Although Hare cites these examples in which factual assertions determine whether a blik is sane or insane, right or wrong, he holds that bliks themselves do not *assert* anything. This seems to be a regrettable conclusion, for reasons that will be given.

A blik, according to some writers, contains or involves tacit or would-be factual assertions, which are either true or false. Others, including Hare, deny this.

The view held and defended here is that a blik may be intended and interpreted, at least in part, as a true or false assertion. A blik may also perform or prompt nonassertive functions, such as worshiping, praying, or singing. According to this view, a blik may be judged by some reference to what it explicitly or implicitly asserts, even though the assertion may not be a stated part of some other-worldly picture.

As to the contention that a blik makes no assertions, it seems strange for a religious or metaphysical believer to say, "I believe in X, but it doesn't really matter to me whether what I believe is true or false." His faith would then rest on nothing at all; it would not differ from lunacy. How can one believe in God without believing that there is a God and without believing whatever associated assertions concerning an afterlife or free will may spring from belief in God? Not all articles of faith are assertions, but how can one contend there are *no* assertions on which a believer depends for the credibility of his faith? How can one rule out all reference to factual assertions or (using Flew's term) "would-be" or disguised assertions? It is difficult, if not impossible, to understand how a person can believe in God without also asserting that God exists. We cannot take him seriously if he denies that the statement "God exists" is true.

A recent writer calls religious bliks "believe-in" statements as distinct from "believe-that" statements. In this way of speaking, other-worldly religious bliks or "believe-in" statements may be reasonably viewed as depending on factual "believe-that" statements.[37] Thus, a blik can be seen as only part-assertive, depending on or involving or presupposing a "would-be" assertion. It may be assessed in relation to the factual assertions on which it depends.

This sort of factual assessment does not differ appreciably from Scheffler's mode of criticizing metaphors, in that a blik may reveal an analogy to be tested. The criticism of analogies that Scheffler introduced for educational metaphors suggests a way to show the role of factual assertions in root metaphors or bliks. One can start choosing among educational bliks by examining what is purportedly asserted or claimed. Assessment of other-worldly bliks by testing their factual analogies or their implied claims for points of possible breakdown may provide good reason for concluding that one educational blik is right and a rival or contradictory blik is wrong.

In this connection one illustration may help. In the eighteenth century William Paley offered a metaphor or blik that exemplifies both the power and the limits of the use of the analogical argument. The topic of the blik is a watch in the desert. Since a watch has properties that evidence a high degree of organization and workmanship, it cannot be supposed that it came into being without a maker. Did it have a maker? Surely. Look next at the universe; see how orderly it is. The universe also has properties that exhibit a high degree of organization and workmanship. Hence, like the watch, it too had to have a maker. The analogical argument is: Just as there is to a watch something that stands in the necessary relationship of watch-maker, there must likewise be, to a universe, someone who is a universe-maker.

If anyone doubts that there is an attempt to make such a connection between metaphysics and education and that this argument in particular has an appeal that affects the teaching of diverse subject matter, he is referred to the following official policy statement on "The Development of Moral and

Spiritual Ideals in the Public Schools," prepared by and for the Board of Education of the City of New York:

> The study of science and mathematics involves a process of discerning order, system, balance and law in the wonderful phenomena of the biological, chemical and physical world. Scientists and mathematicians conceive of the universe as a logical, orderly, predictable place. The vastness and spendor of the heavens, the order and precision of the sun, planets and comets, the marvels of the human body and mind, the beauty of nature, the mystery of photosynthesis, the mathematical structure of the universe, the concept of infinity *cannot do other than lead to humbleness before God's handiwork.*[38]

The ways of rationally criticizing root metaphors or bliks of this kind—by noting the trivial analogies and the limits where they break down—recall a criticism long ago acutely made by Hume.

According to Hume, there is no more reason to compare the making of the world with the work of a machine than to compare it with the growth of a vegetable or a plant. There is no less reason to infer that the world is the product of generation than to infer that it is the result of human-like creation. A watch is made by many hands, while the world is said to be made by God. If the analogy were to be carried out, the world would have to be thought of as made by many gods. But this thought is not what Paley (or the New York City Board of Education) had in mind. The watch-maker metaphor was designed to show that there is *one* maker of the world.

Hume observed that argument by design appeals to experience: the universe is said to resemble things with which we have experience, such as a house or a watch. But on what grounds can we infer that the *cause* of the universe resembles the *cause* of the house or watch? "Is the analogy entire and perfect?" Can one infer the maker of the universe by making more than a guess or a conjecture? To corroborate such reasoning, one must have experienced the origin of the universe. We can all see watches being made before our eyes. But "have worlds ever been formed under your eye?" [39]

There is, moreover, this criticism:

> If you survey a ship, what an exalted idea must we form of the ingenuity of the carpenter who framed so complicated, useful, and beautiful a machine! And what surprise must we feel when we find him a stupid mechanic who imitated others, and copied an art which through a long succession of ages, after multiplied trials, mistakes, corrections, deliberations, and controversies, has been gradually improving. Many worlds might have been botched and bungled throughout an eternity ere this system was struck out; much labor lost; many fruitless trials made; a slow but continued improvement carried on during infinite ages in the art of world-making.[40]

Moreover, how does one know that the world is so orderly as to necessitate its having been constructed by a single maker? What experience have we to demonstrate that the world is basically and predominantly ordered rather than chaotic?

This approach shows how Scheffler's mode of criticizing a metaphor by noting the limits of an analogy may be applied to the evaluation of root metaphors or bliks in education. Although this is not proof of a mathematical kind, it does provide some basis for assessing a metaphysical premise of the sort that Frankena uses: "There is a God" or "There is no God." Hume's criticisms do not imply that there is no God, but they do help us to evaluate an educational policy prescribing what should be taught on the basis of a preconception of the universe as the handiwork of a maker. Hence, a root metaphor or other-worldly blik, as well as the ordinary this-worldly metaphor, is subject to test by rational canons of criticism.

Frankena's use of the theological premise shows the relevance to education of metaphysics and theology when such premises are opened to criticism, but Frankena does not show how these premises are to be criticized. Hence Frankena's argument does not go quite all the way to resolve disagreements among educational policies. On Frankena's grounds alone, metaphysical premises cannot be shown to be sufficient or necessary to justify certain educational conclusions. But extension of Scheffler's criticism of metaphors to theological and metaphysical premises more firmly establishes the relationship of metaphysics to education. The illustrative statement of the New York City Board of Education also shows that, lacking the benefits of rational criticism, educational policies are liable to be constructed without having had any test of their metaphysical and theological assumptions. Such policies might seem to lend weight to contentions that metaphysics is either basically irrelevant to education or else has a special privilege of exemption from criticism while making an impact on philosophy of education. Exclusion of rational appraisal of the metaphysical beliefs bearing on education opens the way to the Capricious notion that any metaphysics or ism may imply any desired educational policy wanted or to the Purist rejoinder that the metaphysical approach to education is absurd, irrelevant, or futile.

The problem that has been considered here begins with the question: Is there a characteristic X distinguishing an educational conclusion that uses metaphysical premises from its contradictory and providing a rational basis for choosing one conclusion over the other? To choose between conclusions, one must choose between a set of premises, MEM, and a contradictory set of premises, ~ MEM. Metaphysics seems by nature to be a difficult area for decision-making. For example, it is not possible to know which metaphysical statement, "God exists," or "God does not exist," is true. But a metaphysical statement may also be expressed as a metaphor or blik. How can one distinguish a right or justifiable blik from a wrong or unjustifiable blik? Are there grounds for saying Blik X is right whereas Blik ~X is wrong?

The procedure for judging metaphysical arguments in education is to look to the conjunction of MEM premises, one of which may allude to a root metaphor or blik. Ways of criticizing metaphors or bliks are helpful to a certain extent in judging metaphysical premises in education.

Following Scheffler's lead, this argument has held that a root metaphor or blik can be criticized by testing the analogy as to whether the intended comparison is of no significance and as to whether it breaks down or is otherwise limited. The result of the test provides a good reason for believing in or acting on one educational metaphor or blik rather than another.

Schematically, the argument may consist of a set of premises MEM, a set of facts, a pedagogical consideration relating MEM's to education, and a practical educational conclusion, which will be called T, for the sake of brevity, meaning "Teach X." MEM's, taken in conjunction with pertinent facts and relevant pedagogical considerations, presumably can help us choose T over some alternative.

On Frankena's grounds, someone else could just as easily advocate other MEM premises, which, when taken in conjunction with relevant facts and pedagogical considerations, would lead to ~T instead of T. The question is, how does one choose between MEM's? It has been suggested here that one must have good reasons for choosing MEM's and a good basis for determining what constitutes the good reasons. Only then could one assert that an opposing set of premises, ~MEM, lacked good reasons. That lack would furnish the basis for deciding not to act on ~T. The determination that each of the MEM premises had good reasons for being believed would be relevant and necessary, though not sufficient by itself, to furnish the basis for deciding to act on the conclusion T, rather than on its contradictory.

As to metaphysical premises, it has been suggested that opening educational metaphors or bliks to analogical criticism can show the reasons for choosing one blik, or part of a blik, over another, A metaphor or blik that has been criticized can count as a basis—unless it is rebutted—for a metaphysical premise. Such testing would quash Paley's metaphor. One way to distinguish a right from a wrong blik is to see whether the blik can stand up to analogical testing of Scheffler's kind. If it can, then it counts as a good reason, although not the only reason, for premising action on the pursuant educational conclusion.

Metaphysical premises, however, are not alone in needing rational assessment. Moral premises are also used to justify educational conclusions, and difficulties occur in deciding the *moral* ends of living and teaching. Moral premises, as well as metaphysical premises, when opened to pertinent criticism, may offer reasons for deciding what should be taught.

A metaphysical belief concerns what the world is like. A moral belief concerns how one ought to live. Both aspects of belief seem necessary, together with pertinent facts and pedagogical considerations, to help us decide what should be taught.

The next chapter will examine the conjunction of other premises—moral, factual, and pedagogical premises that back decisions on what to teach. A close look will be taken at what may count as good reasons for deciding what to teach. The conjunction of good reasons in the premises will presumably give good reasons for the conclusions concerning what should be taught. Such a conclusion, even logically assailable, will be less easily assailable than its contradictory. There may be such overriding motivations for rebutting even good reasons for teaching X that X will continue to be untaught; but there may also be this significance in finding out what "should" be taught—if it is not taught, one can only view that fact *with qualms.*

Looking at the conjunction of other premises to back an educational conclusion will necessitate looking for a criterion by which to distinguish a good reason for a moral premise as well as for criteria by which to assess all good reasons for deciding what should be taught.

There may be much to be said generally against metaphysics in education and in particular against this effort designed to rescue us from the Purist-Capricious impasse. The contention here has been that rational canons of criticism can be employed in the assessment of metaphysical premises, expressed either as metaphors or as bliks. Concerning the metaphysical approach, which has been described by some as a "garrulous absurdity" and irrelevant to boot, it is likely and not easy to reckon with that the sorts of metaphysical views put forward by Thales, Anaximander, Plato, and other early Greeks are ultimately the most important thoughts that it has been in the power of the mind of man to conceive.

1. Cf. Hook, in Chapter II. More recently, Sterling McMurrin has held that "the chief deterrent to progress in philosophy of educa-

tion" rests on the "obstinate" and "futile" assumption that from different metaphysical premises differing educational systems and methods can and should be logically derived ("What about the Philosophy of Education?", *Journal of Philosophy,* LIX, No. 22 [October 25, 1962]). Just as Hook (one may suspect) had his own unannounced form of metaphysical derivation for educational conclusion, so, too, McMurrin has his metaphysical derivation (see Chapter II).

2. William K. Frankena, "McMurrin and Smith on the Philosophy of Education," a paper delivered at the American Philosophical Association Eastern Division Meeting, held in New York City, December, 1962.

3. *Ibid.*

4. The words "obstinate" and "futile" refer to McMurrin's appraisal of the metaphysical approach in education.

5. *Ibid.*

6. *Ibid.*

7. *Ibid.*

8. *Ibid.* Italics added.

9. *Ibid.*

10. This type of implication is a logical implication noted earlier (in Chapter II). It may be recalled that it was said there that a metaphysical premise X *logically* implies an educational conclusion Y when it does so in the sense that Y is *consistent with* X, that Hutchins' emphasis on intellectual virtue did not lead to a stress on a "life-activities" type of curriculum, and that Dewey, who stresses growth, would not stress a Great Books curriculum.

11. Implication is not the same thing as justification (see Chapter V).

12. This could be used to show that philosophy of education (including metaphysics) is essential and not, contrary to Conant, "desirable but unessential." See Conant, *The Education of American Teachers,* p. 131.

13. Frankena, *op. cit.* (note 2 above).

14. One of the hard-earned lessons of analytic philosophy seems to be that metaphysical statements or premises are not true or false in at least the ordinary sense in which we say that "My dog Fido has fleas" is true, or "The Empire State Building is the tallest building in the world" is true. Statements like "Time does not exist" or "The

world is mental or spiritual all over" are not either true or false in the same way, and for this same reason—that we have no way of verifying or falsifying them, that is, of knowing whether they are true or false. But we do have a way of telling whether Fido has fleas and whether the Empire State Building is or isn't the tallest in the world. The metaphysical question is simply too large to answer conclusively in a Purist manner.

15. There are numerous examples in medicine, teaching, food care, engineering, aviation, and the law, which, as a matter of fact, are acceptable without becoming, by implication, therefore justifiable. Practices such as flying in questionable weather pass for "acceptable" without automatically rating the label "justifiable."

16. B. Othanel Smith, "Views on the Role of Philosophy in Teacher Education," *Journal of Philosophy,* LIX (October 25, 1962), 639.

17. *Ibid.* I later show why agreement, in my view, is irrelevant.

18. *Ibid.*

19. *The Language of Education,* p. 48.

20. Smith, *op, cit.*

21. *Ibid.*; and Scheffler, *op. cit.* See also pp. 47–49 for an elaboration of the role and importance of metaphorical or theoretical statements in education. Scheffler goes so far as to suggest a comparison between scientific theory and educational metaphors. "The line, even in science, between serious theory and metaphor, is a thin one, if it can be drawn at all. . . . Limitation is no more reason to reject a metaphor completely than is the fact that there are alternative theories always in itself a reason to reject any given theory in science. A comparison of alternative metaphors may be as illuminating as a comparison of alternative theories, indicating the many-faceted character of the subject."

22. Scheffler, *op. cit.,* p. 48; see also Smith, *op. cit.*

23. For an extended treatment of educational metaphors, see Scheffler, *op. cit.,* pp. 47–59. A consideration of root metaphors or picture-preferences in education, as Scheffler has shown, is undoubtedly a theoretically fruitful way of suggesting insightful comparisons between well-known things and processes and those that are less well known. It is only when this is taken too literally, and when the application of a metaphor is unrestrictedly overextended, that it may be false and cease to be illuminating.

24. The above account is heavily indebted to Scheffler and to B. Othanel Smith. The latter was the first to make use of "root metaphors" in education.

Most metaphors depict the child. Dewey, however, besides developing the growth metaphor, speaks of the school as the "embryo of society," and elsewhere compares education in social life to renewal in biological life. "What nutrition and reproduction are to physiological life, education is to social life." John Dewey, *Democracy and Education* (New York: Macmillan, 1917), p. 11. See also Scheffler, *op. cit.*, for a more detailed discussion of educational metaphors that are not intended as metaphysically basic or root metaphors.

25. Thus educational metaphors, in being used to guide and recommend a given curriculum proposal, also perform imperative or deliberative and affective functions intended to coax, goad, guide, inspire, move, impel, educationists to act. Since in any school program a practical choice has to be made, this choice is not made without (tacitly) preferring one educational metaphor over another; nor, however, is this choice made without considering the educational proposal which is attached to the metaphor (as a sort of rider on a contract).

26. See, for example, Joe Burnett, "Observations on the Logical Implications of Philosophic Theory for Educational Theory and Practice," *Educational Theory,* XI (April, 1961), 65–70.

27. The YMCA picture of an ideally educated Christian, for example, presumably differs from an Ethical Culture Humanist's, and so presumably will the proposed curriculum of either, to the extent that is needed for it to be consistent with its avowed beliefs.

28. From "Basic Issues in American Secondary Education—1956" by B. Othanel Smith, in *Frontiers of Secondary Education I,* edited by Paul M. Halverson. Copyright © 1956 by Syracuse University Press, Syracuse, New York.

29. For the same reason that Frankena's Judeo-Christian example is neither necessary nor sufficient to justify the teaching of obedience to God *at large.*

30. *Op. cit.* Even if consensus were achievable as to what society ought to be, that would not imply that a consensus ought to be the basis for answering the question of educational purposes; there was, after all, a time when consensus as to the flatness of the earth was thought to imply that the earth was flat. (See Chapter III, pp. 72–75, for an elaboration of this point.) The lack of consensus, moreover, does not show that some aims of education cannot be shown to be better

than others, nor therefore, that the problem of deciding educational purposes need necessarily be perennial; nor does Smith show, finally, that philosophical attention to the aims of education deserves to be disparaged. (I have tried to show why not on pages 105–9 of this chapter.)

31. *Ibid.*

32. *Ibid.*

33. Scheffler, *op. cit.*, p. 52.

34. Stephen C. Pepper, *World Hypotheses* (Berkeley: University of California Press, 1948), pp. 91–92.

35. Hereafter, the word "blik" will, for notational convenience and ease, be written without quotes or italics.

36. See, for example, Flew and MacIntyre (eds.), *New Essays in Philosophical Theology,* pp. 96–130.

37. Ralph Sleeper, "The 'Meaning of Life' Question: Linguistic Philosophy and Religious Belief," *Cross Currents,* XIV (Summer, 1964). Sleeper denies that "believe-in" statements depend (logically) on "believe-that" statements. Kai Nielsen, Flew, Passmore, Horsburgh, and Blackstone, however, disagree with this view. The question of whether bliks (or "believe-in" statements) logically depend upon "believe-that" statements (or what amounts to the same thing, factual assertions) continues to be debated. See for example, W. Blackstone, *The Problem of Religious Knowledge* (Englewood Cliffs, N. J.: Prentice-Hall, 1963), especially Chapters VI and VII. A strong thought (with a possible commission of the *ad ignorantiam* fallacy) is voiced by D. J. O'Connor: "If a religion is true and can be shown to be so, then it should be taught. . . . And if it cannot be shown to be true, then it ought not to be propagated officially . . . " (*An Introduction to Philosophy of Education,* p. 135). I myself confess that I find it logically odd for a believer to say, "I am committed to religious belief X, but I don't care if it's true or false"; for his faith would come to rest on nothing at all and not differ appreciably from lunacy.

38. Adopted in 1956. Italics added.

39. David Hume, *Dialogues Concerning Natural Religion,* ed. Henry D. Aiken (New York: Hafner, 1948), Part II, p. 25.

40. *Ibid.*, Part V, p. 39.

V. The Place of Moral Reasons in Education

Thoughts without content are empty;
intuitions without concepts are blind.

—IMMANUEL KANT

Some arguments in philosophy of education purport to guide educational programs and policies from a moral point of view. Much can be said for the legitimacy of that aim. Metaphysical arguments and issues may often appear too abstruse, too abstract, too remote from education, or even too unresolvable to invite public or professional interest. Some philosophers of education may have little propensity for the supposedly deeper metaphysical subtleties and hence may elect to banish metaphysics once and for all. Not for them the terrors of the metaphysical jungle!

There are those who see a special relevance of moral arguments to education and would rather try to work out the relationship between morals and education than attempt to tread the more tenuous path between metaphysics and education.[1]

Moreover, the moral (rather than the metaphysical) goals of a society are often quite directly expressed as the goals of education,[2] and these influence educational policies and presumably lend direction to the operation of school systems, giving authority to educational programs.

Moral issues impinge upon what is euphemistically called in education "The Great Debate"—whether to construct school buildings that cost more money; whether to bus children; whether to give scholarships only to the gifted; and what educational programs to conduct for teachers.

Since moral practices concern the good or harm that people do to each other—and there is a great deal of good or harm that can come from schooling—the daily and continuing moral role of the schools cannot be overestimated. Gilbert Ryle has reminded us that moral questions are an everyday affair; one need not tie a string around one's finger to remember the existence of moral problems.

Moral problems and moral arguments, therefore, have an urgency that their metaphysical counterparts seem to lack. Even though the schools may remain open while we debate metaphysics, they may not be able to stay open—witness, in some instances, the South—when we disagree sharply on our moral purposes. Debates on moral ideals do press directly on educational policies and programs, and so we may well look for rational canons or criticism for assessing moral arguments in education.

Moral arguments have an even more general bearing on education. The age-old problem that Plato presented, of how we ought to live, is answered in part by how, morally, we educate the young.

The notion of bliks seemed appropriate for expressing metaphysical premises leading to decisions on what should be taught to the young. It is clear that an educational blik, expressing an ideal for the education of young people in relation to society, to the universe, and to their ultimate destiny, affects the principles by which we bring up our children. There are writers who deny the relationship between metaphysics and morals, but it is hard to understand how a man can live by moral principles that prescribe what ought to be and yet not have some metaphysical or theological view of whether there is a God or the Idea of the Good. Such a view would establish a connection, by way of moral principles, between the idea of the other-worldly, or its rejection, and the world of man. It would thus include the direction, content, and method of the education of man. That, at any rate, is what constitutes the once-respected, traditional conception of the synoptic and visionary function of philosophy.

The world view, or "root metaphor," or blik triggers a program of action to fulfil the ideal. It sets up the target—the final or ultimate purpose or end of education. The moral principle that is consistent with the metaphysical ideal suggests a program of action designed to bring about the ideal (Hutchins' or Dewey's, for example). A moral principle may, itself, be seen as the purpose or end of education, with the educational program of action proposed as a means to that end. This relation between metaphysical and moral ends and means seems not to be an untoward extension of Dewey's means-ends continuum. For most teachers, the metaphysical view or root assumption is put out of sight, and soon educators come to think that only moral principles provide the ends of education.

The metaphysical blik or root metaphor triggers, prods, or inspires a moral, intellectual, and physical program of education for bringing up the young. In Braithwaite's felicitous phrase, the blik is "a spring of action" for the moral and educational program.

The idea that moral and educational principles are validly derived from a metaphysical view is logically assailable, and the connection certainly should be subjected to rational criticism. But that the metaphysical view does give rise to moral principles, and these in turn to educational principles, is illustrated by the derivation from Thomism of the moral principles contained in the Ten Commandments, prescribing an agapeistic way of life in the education of the young and the conduct of the elders. The fact that isms may be seriously criticized in philosophy does not mean that they are not "philosophies of education."

The commandment "Thou shalt not kill" as expressed in the Old Testament would not need to be obeyed apart from acceptance of some conception of God. Some writers hold that the moral principle proscribing murder is rationally defensible without commitment to a conception of God. But it would not then be the Fifth Commandment backed by the Old Testament theological blik.

Whether moral principles are logically or otherwise independent of metaphysics continues to be debated in philosophy and in educational philosophy. There seems to be an uneasy ease in asserting that there is or is not a relation between metaphysics and education. The far harder task is to tell *what* the relation is or is not. Following Frankena's lead and, from another direction, Scheffler's and Smith's, this study has attempted to show how metaphysics and education are related and that, at least psychologically, people are apt to derive their moral principles from a metaphysical or theological world view, no matter how crude and inexplicit it may be. The well-known philosopher J. C. C. Smart confirms this view by saying:

> As we shall see, and as has been generally recognized in modern philosophy, it is not possible to deduce propositions about what ought to be done purely from propositions about what is the case. It follows that the principles of conduct are by no means unambiguously determined by our general philosophy. Nevertheless, in their laudable objection to those who would deduce ethics from the nature of the world (and in particular to some of those biologists who would base ethics on the theory of evolution and the like), philosophers have tended to obscure the fact that our general philosophical and scientific beliefs may strongly influence our ethical principles. For example, if one of our principles of conduct were that we should do what is commanded by a personal God, and if our world view were one which left no place for such a God, then this principle of conduct would have to be given up, or at least we should have to find some other reason for adhering to it. . . . The example of theology was brought up simply to show in a vivid way that metaphysics can be relevant to ethics. We must certainly not jump from the impossibility of deducing "ought" from "is" to the untenable position that our general philosophical and scientific views have no bearing on our ethical ones.[3]

One can go further than Smart by suggesting that there is some merit to Frankena's notion that the conjunction of metaphysical, epistemological, and metamoral (MEM) premises, together with relevant facts, would be necessary to justify a decision as to what should be taught. It may well be that MEM's, taken either together or singly, are needed in order to decide upon purposes of education—a decision that affects the formation of policies governing content and method.

Since the purposes of education—whether metaphysical or moral—continue to be debated, canons of criticism seem to be needed to assess the arguments and so to provide a way out of the Purist-Capricious impasse. Under consideration next will be how moral arguments, whether or however they depend upon a metaphysical view, can be rationally assessed.

The Teaching of Knowledge, Skills, and Attitudes

We sometimes speak of teaching knowledge, skills, and attitudes because we find it convenient to distinguish between teaching Johnny that the earth is round, teaching him to drive a car, and teaching him to be truthful. Somewhat after the pattern of Ryle, we might describe the first of these as "teaching-that," the second as "teaching-how," and the third, which does not derive from Ryle's distinction, as "teaching-for." The last of these, the teaching of attitudes, is the most difficult among all teaching jobs and the one most likely to be a "task." Try as hard as we may to teach for the development of attitudes, we do not always succeed; it takes more training, ingenuity, and effort to teach attitudes than to teach either knowledge or skills.

In the curriculum it is easy to see the specific courses about which we can all debate, but it is not so easy to see the most hidden attitudes for which we are likely to teach. The courses, for example, in a public school may seem very much like those taught in a private school. And although there may not be a single explicit statement in either school on the subject of equality or privilege, the twelve years of exposure to either a public or private school exercises a considerable influence on a child's attitudes toward these questions. Attitudes thus shaped are not likely to be seriously altered by anything that happens thereafter.

Even though attitudes are more difficult to teach than either knowledge or skills, attitudes presumably provide the principal reason for teaching knowledge and skills. Then how do the attitudes for which we teach guide our choice of what knowledge and skills to teach?

When the question of what to teach is asked philosophically, it is not quite like the question of what items to select in trimming a defense budget or in screening college applicants, where the answer lies in applying correctly established criteria. The questions, for example, of whether we should teach a Victorian or a Freudian version of *Hamlet* or whether we should teach a democratic or a communist version of society cannot be answered in terms of money or space limitation. Nor are answers found by making some abstraction from what there is to know or by pruning down available resources in the culture, on the grounds that one cannot teach everything. A fundamental, evaluative argument that is intended to answer the question "What shall be taught?" calls for a rational choice among our values, in so far as we have to choose one way of life (or one *part* of a way of life, or some attitude or value or blik) over another.[4] Once the issue has been made clear, in the sense that the alternatives are mutually exclusive, we cannot choose both, or part of both, because we cannot teach our children to live simultaneously as good Christians, good Mau Mau's, good dialectical materialists, and good democrats. The attitudes for which we teach, to the extent they reflect a way of life that is incompatible with some other way of life, include certain areas of knowledge and of skill, and exclude others. To choose the strictly fundamentalist Christian way of life, for example, would render inconsistent the teaching of the knowledge and skills required to understand biologic evolution. Thus, the way of life by which we choose to live, as reflected in the attitudes for which we teach, sets the standard for determining what knowledge and skills to teach.

Then for what way of life and for what attitudes or values shall we teach? Although the question "For what shall we teach?" also raises the question of what knowledge and skills to teach, the main consideration now is the type of argument that would answer the question concerning attitudes. What knowledge and skills to teach may, at least in part, be inferred from the attitudes sought. (See the notion of "logical implication" in education, in Chapters II and IV.)

The type of argument to answer the question about attitudes would make use of good reasons for backing one conclusion as against another. The question "What shall be taught?" is regarded here as a particular instance of the general moral and evaluative question. It therefore has features in common with the moral or evaluative question. Consideration of it shows how both moral and metaphysical premises may be pertinent to deciding what to teach and also what distinctive characteristics the evaluative argument has. These characteristics would be grossly handled if one were to study a straightforward moral or metaphysical argument on the assumption that an argument for metaphysical or moral conclusions automatically (or deductively) implied or justified a conclusion to an evaluative argument in education. The question posed by Spencer that we noted in Chapter I, for example, is neither through the efforts of metaphysics nor through those of morals *sui generis* answered by an argument in Sense II.

The Use of Good Reasons in Deciding What Shall Be Taught

When a speaker says, "X should be taught," one may start with the assumption, which can be later withdrawn, that he has good reasons for believing so. The speaker can use the good reasons to imply his conclusion concerning what shall be taught. If a speaker says, for example, that patriotism should be taught, one may assume he has good reasons for that conclusion. Among them may be this (abbreviated as Q_1):

M_1 Attitudes that serve the national interest should be taught.

I_1 Patriotism (is an attitude that) serves the national interest.

T_1 Therefore, patriotism should be taught.[5]

The reasons offered for teaching patriotism include the Instrumental Principle, I, which asserts that what is taught is an appropriate instrumentality toward an end. The moral principle, M, may also stand for the conjunction of MEM's. I, as a means to some end, is a contingent empirical premise dependent for its truth on what happens in the world. As such, it is open to empirical falsification. If I is falsified, then it is withdrawn as a good reason for deciding to act on T; it is the actual falsification and not the openness to falsification of I that counts against it as a good reason for acting on T.

Without a contingent premise, the argument would be empty.[6] While the contingent premise may count as a good reason for teaching patriotism, the mere presence of I is not sufficient in a practical syllogism to imply that patriotism should be taught. The reason for this is not hard to see. In conformity with the second of the rules elucidated by R. M. Hare, that "no imperative conclusion can be validly drawn from a set of premises which does not contain at least one imperative premise," at least one of the premises in a practical syllogism must be imperative.[7] Since the conclusion T_1 is an imperative and I is not an imperative, M must be an imperative in order for the conclusion to be valid. Without an imperative in M, no conclusion of the form T can be validly drawn; the presence of an imperative in M is a necessary condition to imply validly a conclusion of the form T.

Regardless of whether M_1 or I_1 is true or false (or neither), as long as Hare's condition has been fulfilled by the presence of an imperative, the premises taken together validly imply the conclusion T_1. Since there is, moreover, a contingent premise, the argument (abbreviated Q_1) is non-empty.

Satisfaction of the conditions of logical validity and of a non-empty argument is not, however, synonymous with having good reasons for deciding to act on T. While neither of the premises has to be true in order for the conclusion to be valid (see Chapter I, section on Smullyan), both must be true for the conclusion to be *sound*. If I is false, it is not a good reason to decide that one ought to act on T.

Even when I is true and M is an imperative premise, a difficulty exists. An opposing speaker can use the contrary of M_1 ($\sim M_1$) along with I_1 to imply $\sim T_1$ (abbreviated $\sim Q_1$). Depending on whether we start from M_1 or $\sim M_1$, in combination with I_1, the conclusion T_1 or $\sim T_1$ will follow logically. Then how does the presence of (some) good reasons help us to choose between contradictory conclusions, both purporting to answer the question "What shall be taught?" The presence of a logically good reason (Hare's second rule) in the form of an imperative premise and the presence of a factually good reason in the form of a true contingent premise —both necessary to draw a valid and sound conclusion T_1— do not help us to decide between T_1 and $\sim T_1$. The presence of (some) good reasons can accordingly be used to decide either for T_1 or for $\sim T_1$, depending on whether one begins with M_1 or $\sim M_1$. But how do we choose between M_1 and $\sim M_1$?

An argument of form Q performs a genuine choice-guiding function between contradictory alternatives, then, if it not only implies a valid conclusion of the form T but also gives us good reasons to justify our deciding to act on T rather than $\sim T$.

If the argument is valid, the premises are justified, the reasons in the premises justify the conclusion T, and a justified conclusion is one that I ought to act on, then I have good reason to decide to act on T.

One may therefore say of an argument like this, "You have a valid argument for T_1 and since, in addition, your reasons (among which are M_1 and I_1) are good, then you have good reason for deciding to act on T_1." But it is unnerving in this instance, even though the argument is valid, to accept the conclusion as justified and therefore as a conclusion on which we ought to act.[8]

It is perfectly plausible and logical to say to someone about an argument like Q_1, "You have given us good reasons for teaching X, but we ought not to teach it." If asked "Why?" we can say, "The good reasons you gave for teaching X, all things considered, do not add up to *a good enough reason* for teaching X, even though your argument is both logically valid and non-empty, and even though it may seem logically odd or out of place—but not logically self-contradictory—to decide that we shouldn't teach X."

One way of gauging whether it is logically odd to add, "But we shouldn't teach X," is to ask, "Why should we decide that X is *worth* teaching?" The task is then to answer this type of "Why?" question with, if not the best reason, at least a good enough reason for deciding that X should be taught instead of $\sim X$ or Y or Z or any other logically incompatible alternative that conflicts with X. It is important to distinguish a good reason from one that, while it is good, is not *good enough.* An argument of this kind performs an evaluative choice-guiding function by giving us a good enough reason to choose X over $\sim$X.

What counts as a good enough reason to choose between two contradictory conclusions in answer to the question "What shall be taught?" It counts if all the reasons in M and I of an argument Q can be shown to be good reasons (and if, correspondingly, at least one among an opposing set of reasons fails to qualify as good), and if an argument of the form Q takes account of, and is relevant to, the practice of teaching (unlike an opposing argument). The justification of the premises, although it provides a good reason for the justification of the conclusion, does not by itself provide a good enough reason for deciding that we should act on T. What is needed is a good reason to show that the conclusion T, in addition to being justified, is relevant to the practice of teaching. We have a good enough reason to act on a given conclusion T, then, when the argument is logically valid, when there is at least a true contingent premise, making the argument non-empty, when the premises are justified, and when there is a good reason why a given conclusion T is relevant.

A good enough reason for choosing between two contradictory conclusions that reply to the question "What should be taught?" is proposed in the following example (abbreviated Q_2):

M_2 True accounts of the origin of human life on earth should be taught.

I_2 The theory of evolution is a true account of the origin of human life on earth.

T_2 Therefore, the theory of evolution should be taught.

To show that this type of argument presents a good enough reason for teaching the theory of evolution, three conditions will be discussed: one applies to M, another to I, and a third has to do with the practical relevance of the conclusion.[9]

The Moral Principle

What is the difference between Q_1 and Q_2? In Q_1 we have a good reason to imply T_1, but we do not have a good enough reason to decide to act on T_1 (and correspondingly a good enough reason to decide not to act on $\sim T_1$). In Q_2, on the other hand, we have a good enough reason logically to imply T_2 and also to choose to act on T_2 (and refuse to act on $\sim T_2$). How is this so?

In both arguments, I is falsifiable. Hence, we have the possibility of depending on or withdrawing I as a good reason.[10] If either I_1 or I_2 were falsified, we would have to withdraw it as a good reason for deciding to act on T. And if we had to withdraw it as a good reason when it was falsified, then it would not be a good enough reason to decide the question of whether to act on T rather than $\sim T$.

We know on what grounds—verification—we can count I as a good reason. But what are the grounds for counting or withdrawing M as a good reason? R. M. Hare skilfully set up two rules for the application of logic to moral inferences.

It is now suggested that this third rule be added: *There is a good enough reason for deciding to act on an imperative conclusion T only when all the premises are universal (in M and in I).* This rule finds ample support in a general theorem of the formal syllogism, which states that "if one premise is particular, the conclusion must also be particular." [11] For the conclusion T to be universal, both premises M and I have to be universal; if M or I is particular, then the conclusion must be particular. Since the conclusion T is universal and I is universal, M also has to be universal; if it is not, then it must be withdrawn as a good reason. Once M has been withdrawn as a good reason, premise I, which remains intact, does not count as a good enough reason for deciding between the two contradictory conclusions, T and $\sim$T.

What makes M either a particular or a universal premise? We know that a metaphysical premise such as "All men are mortal" is universal from looking at the universal quantifier "all." But what are the characteristics of a universal moral premise? If there is any sense in which moral principles count as universal premises in value-implying syllogisms, it seems to be in the sense that premises are capable of becoming universal and thus can be said to be "universalizable."

In its original formulation, the universalizability principle referred to Kant's categorical imperative "Act only on that maxim whereby thou canst at the same time will that it should become a universal law." [12] Kant used the example of "promise-keeping" to show the moral necessity of affirming universal or U-type valuations. If there were no moral obligations to keep promises, the idea of making promises "would become impossible," and the moral action of wilfully breaking a promise would, Kant said, "necessarily contradict itself." [13] Later, Kant applied the universal law of our own rational making, which he believed necessary to a logical basis for ethics. If universalizability could be named a necessary characteristic of ethical statements and the minimal sense in which a moral statement could be called true, then it would be self-contradictory for a "good will" to deny a universal moral principle such as promise-keeping or truth-telling. A moral statement could be said to be true if denial of the statement would be self-contradictory; it would be logically impossible to express our rational will and at the same time to deny a universal law of our own rational making.

In recent formulations, first by E. A. Gellner and then by Hare, a U-type valuation is distinguished from an E-type valuation. (U-type may be associated with the concept of universal and E-type with the existentialist focus on the individual.) According to Gellner, E-type valuations contain "ineliminable" references to individuals, whereas U-type valuations contain "eliminable" references to individuals. Examples of the first are "selfishness, romantic love, loyalty; of the second . . . , the impartial judgments of a judge." [14] Since individual reference is ineliminable in connection with patriotism, it is not possible, according to Gellner, to be a U-type patriot.

In adopting Gellner's distinction, Hare accepts the principle of the eliminability of singular terms in U-type valuations but argues that while maxims may be E-type or U-type, all moral reasons are U-type. According to Hare, the notion that there are E-type moral valuations comes from misunderstanding the moral use of the word "ought" and from "not distinguishing non-moral imperatives from moral imperatives." [15] Hare goes on to make the stronger claim that *all* moral valuations are universalizable and that *there are no E-type moral valuations.*

This study does not make Hare's stronger claim that all moral valuations are U-type, but does support his other claim that universal moral premises are U-type. There are undoubtedly differences between Gellner and Hare and also between the recent formulations and the earlier Kantian formulation of universalizability. The position here is that any universal moral premises in value-implying syllogisms are U-type; that a characteristic of U-type valuations is the eliminability of singular terms therein; and that the use of U-type valuations, limited though it may be, can provide a good reason for denying opposing non–U-type valuations. The intention here is to show that use of a U-type valuation as a good reason to deny an opposing U-type valuation need not be self-contradictory.

To apply the E- or the U-type distinction to M, one can often tell whether M is particular or universal by looking at its terms, such as "national interest." According to Gellner's notion, if the singularity in M_1 is ineliminable, then M_1 is E-type.

Which, if either, use of M (M_1 or M_2) is particularizable? Which, if either, is universalizable? There is no absoluteness to this distinction. The use of M_1 seems more nearly to resemble an E-type valuation, and the use of M_2 seems more nearly to resemble a U-type valuation.

If the use of M_1 to back the conclusion "Patriotism should be taught" is restricted to the partisan use—one in which particularity is ineliminable—then M_1 is not universal and must be withdrawn as a good reason for T_1. Although the other reasons in the argument may remain intact, withdrawal of M means they are no longer good enough reasons to act on T_1.

Application of the third rule requiring universal moral premises for imperative conclusions makes it of the first importance to distinguish particularity from universality. Without a mark of universality or of particularity, like "the national interest" or "patriotism," one cannot tell whether M is a universal premise. If M is not universal (and it seems not, in M_1), then it does not support an evaluative argument in education leading to a decision to act either on T_1 or $-T_1$. Without universality in M, the totality of the premises among which M is found cannot count as a good enough reason for deciding either to act on T_1 or to act on $-T_1$.

What is the test of whether M_1 or M_2 is universalizable? Consider first the ineliminability of "the national interest" as a singular term in contrast to "True accounts of the origin of human life on earth." Although "the origin of life on earth" is singular, nevertheless, in the principle invoked—to "teach true accounts" as opposed to false accounts—its singularity is eliminable. If the appeal in M_1 is only to partisan assent, particularly concerning some special privilege that is ineliminable, what we then have is, not a moral principle, but an ideological principle—which, in expressing partisan allegiance, is not universalizable.[16]

Consider next the function of a universalizable principle in denying an opposing valuation. It is perfectly plausible, for example, to take exception to (or to deny) M_1, since there is not a universal moral reason for saying that we should or should not teach attitudes that serve the national interest.

M_2, however, being universalizable, gives at least one good reason for deciding to act on T_2. To deny M_2 is, in a sense, to say that we ought to teach falsehood; but the idea of teaching falsehood, which ordinarily contains ineliminable singular terms,[17] is not universalizable and therefore cannot count as a good moral reason for affirming the contrary of M_2 ($\sim M_2$). It is not necessarily, however, self-contradictory to deny M_2, nor is it logically impossible to deny or reject any U-type valuation. Notice of universality warns against frivolous rejection of U-type valuations, for universality is ordinarily, it seems, a good reason—though not the only reason—for affirming a moral valuation.

Imagine, though, that someone says U-type valuations are a priori. It has been noted that to identify a collective attitude like "consensus" with morality amounts to ignoring the difference between "is" and "ought," for one can apply the open-question argument to it without self-contradiction. One could say: "You identify consensus with morality, and you say that a decision K was consensually arrived at. But was K morally right? Would it be self-contradictory to say that K was morally wrong? It may be no more than possible that K was morally wrong. But so long as that is logically possible, then consensus is not a synonym of morality."

A recent writer shows how even U-type valuations can be rejected:

> . . . These definitions must be rejected. . . . "Right" does not mean the same as "in accord with nature" or "consistently universalizable," because it makes sense to ask, "This act is in accord with nature, but is it right?" and "This act is consistently universalizable, but is it right?" Even if the answer is always "no," it is still a sensible—that is non-self-contradictory—question to ask. "Right" cannot mean the same thing as any one of these other expressions, else there would be no controversy . . . as to whether everything that fulfills the criterion in question is also right. If any of these proffered definitions were acceptable, then arguing about them pro or con would be as pointless as arguing whether a yard is three feet. Those who asserted that it was would be defending a tautology, and those who denied it would be saying something self-contradictory.[18]

A U-type valuation may be rejected or denied without self-contradiction by being qualified in one of several ways. For example, "Tell the truth" may become "Tell the truth—except when doing so would endanger human life." Exceptive clauses of this kind show that a U-type valuation may be rejected or denied in everyday practical application to particular moral acts. There may, for example, be two U-type valuations that contradict each other in terms of called-for simultaneous action. For instance, "You should keep promises, and so you should return this book now as you promised," as opposed to, "I should be considerate of human life and so I should care now for my dying mother who needs me." Here the two U-type valuations are incompatible in application. Since I can do only one of the things called for by these valuations, I may, without self-contradiction, reject or deny the first by saying: "I agree that I should keep promises and return this book, but my dying mother needs me. I should place priority on consideration of human life over keeping a promise. Therefore, instead of returning the book, I should go to my mother."

An exceptive clause denies the application of a U-type valuation; in the foregoing instance, it is by reference to another U-type valuation rather than to a non–U-type valuation.

If the foregoing instance may be used to indicate something about M, then when I is U-type, it counts against a non–U-type statement, such as M_1. Although the denial of M_2 is not self-contradictory, a universal moral premise can be denied or rejected only by some other U-type valuation that is overriding. Suppose, for example, that someone says, "Lying is wrong," and someone else says, "He lied, but he was not acting wrongly." The second statement is the contradictory of the first and denies or rejects it—unless there is a good reason for the affirmation "He was not acting wrongly." What could it be? One may have a good reason for the affirmation if one appeals to a U-type moral valuation, "Saving lives is right," and asserts, "In this case the only way to save a life was to lie." Thus, "He lied, but was not acting wrongly" appeals for its good reason to a U-type valuation. A U-type valuation has been denied or rejected in this instance—but only by another U-type valuation. Thus, if M is U-type and there is a good moral reason to reject or deny its application to a given (teaching) act, then M may not have priority among all U-type valuations, but its denial is not the denial of all U-type valuations.

U-type principles, then, are deniable—but not by non–U-type (or E-type) principles. In the sense indicated above, even exceptional applications are U-type. A further difficulty arises if two U-type statements in M are pitted against each other, and neither becomes an exceptive clause to reject or deny the other. Then neither is a good reason against the other or even against an opposing T statement—unless there are non-moral reasons for acting on one conclusion rather than another. The practical application of a U-type statement in M, as M is used along with other reasons, provides a further indirect way for a U-type statement in M to be rejected or denied on good grounds, as in Sense II.

There is another way by which M, if universalizable, may be denied. It is logically possible, for example, to imagine that the truth about the world is so bad that everyone who is taught the truth is led to panic and suicide (the foregoing true statement being the sole exception). The only life that is humanly endurable is thus a life of illusions and falsehoods.[19] If teaching falsehood in such a world would prevent panic and suicide, it could be argued that would be a good reason for teaching falsehood; the prevention of panic and mass suicide is an alternative U-type valuation, which might, under such circumstances (without self-contradiction) take moral precedence over teaching the truth and constitute an overriding reason for not teaching the truth.

The greater empirical likelihood that teaching falsehood—except in so hypothetical and far-fetched a situation—would lead to the breakdown of society, at least as we care to live in it, may be adduced as a reason for teaching the truth.

The idea of not teaching the truth is ordinarily reprehensible to us, and in the absence of an exceptional circumstance such as the foregoing fantasy, there is considerable oddness about denying that we should teach the truth. Yet the denial of M_2, though odd, is not self-contradictory. It is possible to argue, whether rightly or wrongly, that the avoidance of panic and suicide is a good reason for teaching illusion and falsehood instead of truth. M_2, therefore, can theoretically be rejected or denied without self-contradiction. But without some defensible exceptive, or what H. L. A. Hart terms a "defeasible clause," there is good reason against affirming that we should teach falsehood. The logical possibility of denying M_2 by some other conflicting U-type statement does not, however, mean that there is every good reason to deny M_2 as there seems to be for denying M_1. It does border on the grotesque to imagine our teaching—on the basis of a conclusion arrived at through arguments—falsehood instead of truth. Still, the desirability of teaching falsehood under extraordinary circumstances can and ought to be considered; such a possibility makes arguments against M_2, however odd, not self-contradictory.

A U-type valuation counts as a good reason for affirming a moral decision and hence for deciding what should be taught. The universalizability of any U-type valuation is not, however, defined as moral in the way that a yard is defined as three feet. Universalizability is a good reason for, but not a definition of, what ought to be taught.

Some formidable arguments have been put forward recently to suggest that not all moral valuations are U-type. Even assuming the desirability of performing U-type acts—great moral deeds done by saints and heroes—such acts of supererogation,[20] although *desiderated*, may be held not to be universalizable (E-type rather than U-type), for such acts are rare or unique.

The acts of saints and heroes certainly go beyond U-type obligations, and their acts are singular, not universal, in fact. Nevertheless, the *desideratum* intended by those who teach or tell about such acts is wider emulation. Universalizability is, after all, not synonymous with nose-counting. Even if heroic and saintly acts are not expected to be emulated—or *imitated* (Plato's word for it)—by all people, such acts, having the highest moral marks, are ideally *desiderated* by all, so long as they have (on Kantian grounds) a rational will. "Would that rare and exceptional saintly and heroic virtues could be taught" must have been the cry of every post-Plato moral pedagogue whose will and aim has been to engage in the teaching of something rare and exceptionally desirable, once called virtue.

The hope implicit in recounting the acts of saints and heroes is that, were we of their moral mettle and in their circumstances, we too would feel that we ought to do likewise. We are not less men for failing to do likewise, but by this failure, we fail morally to become great men. We are told the story of the hero and the saint in the hope that we may, wherever possible, emulate (or imitate) the exceptionally desirable act. It is not any less desirable for being repeated less often. Civilizations have fallen just because there was a dearth of outstanding moral acts at precisely the times of need.

The good act is unique; the intention of recounting it is to inspire us to consider following the example. Aristotle held that if one wants to know what is good, it is best to follow the example of a good man. There can be only one Socrates, one Gandhi, one Giordano Bruno, one Martin Luther King; but heroic acts of the kind they performed can and ought to be done over again. The *desiderated* repeatability of saintly and heroic acts attests to their universalizability. The exemplary act against some evil or wrong ennobles the doer and exhorts us to follow. That we do not have it in us to do likewise makes the exemplary act no less worthy of reiteration. The difficult task of morally educating more people to do likewise seems less impossible because the exemplary act has been performed. Moral education gets its impetus from the spirited acts that are sometimes told in history books and sometimes in fairy tales. Spinoza may have had a similar thought when, at the end of the *Ethics,* he wrote:

> If the way which, as I have shown, leads hither seems very difficult, it can nevertheless be found. It must indeed be difficult since it is so seldom discovered for if salvation lay ready to hand and could be discovered without great labor, how could it be possible that it should be neglected almost by everybody? But all things noble are as difficult as they are rare.

The saintly and heroic act is thus not in every sense E-type. In the intentional sense, "would that more teachers would teach and live and die like Socrates" is not the kind of valuation to be dismissed as unworthy. The will, the intention, the appeal that Socrates' example might be made manifold—it is these that make this judgment universalizable. When we hear of similar moral courage, we are inspired to applaud and to follow—witness the heroic examples of Giordano Bruno and, more recently, of John T. Scopes of Tennessee.

Even if we cannot teach people to emulate great and rare moral acts in all instances, because of the recalcitrance of "human nature," we nevertheless can and do and should teach people to give their wholehearted approval and support to heroic and saintly deeds. And we should correspondingly teach disapproval of the acts of cowards, scoundrels, and sinners. In the sense of appeal to the morality of mankind, the acts of the hero and the saint are U-type.

We cannot all be Socrates, Scopes, Gandhi, Giordano Bruno; but (to extend a point made by Charles Stevenson) we can be educated to feel approval and support for them in their exemplary acts—and, to the extent of our ability, to emulate them.

There is, of course, a great gap between approving of others for throwing themselves on hand grenades to save their fellows and doing such a deed oneself. We ought therefore to will that we ourselves, in circumstances corresponding to those of saints or heroes, would not only approve of great acts but would do likewise.

Against the notion that an act of supererogation is E-type because it is performed only once, one must emphasize that the intention of its being praised is that it be universally approved, supported, imitated. In the potential infinitude of approval, support, and emulation, even the supererogatory act of the saint or the hero is universalizable.

Universalizing supererogatory acts puts us on the trail toward affirmatively answering the question of whether virtue can be taught. Without universalizability, moral grounds for deciding what should be taught seem to be undercut.

To sum up so far: a good reason for affirming M is that it is U-type; this counts also as a good reason for denying the contrary of M; a U-type valuation need not be regarded as logically undeniable; a U-type valuation may be denied or rejected if qualified by an exceptive clause, but it is not deniable by a non–U-type valuation. Thus a U-type valuation like M_2 counts as a good reason for affirmation and as a good reason against its contrary $\sim M_2$ ("We should teach untrue accounts"). The presence of a U-type valuation does not, however, make it logically self-contradictory to deny M_2. The denial of the U-type valuation by a U-type exceptive clause may count as a good reason against M_2. There may be nonmoral reasons for deciding against T_2 (teaching evolution), but to reject M_2 by saying, "We should teach untruth," without an unusually good reason, has a false ring. In a similar connection, Ryle observes that "the oddness, if it exists" in such an idea as teaching falsehood "might be one source of the strength of the notion of the Moral Law." [21]

Yet the Moral Law need not be airtight. The possibility of denying a universal moral principle in some such way as qualification with an exceptive clause is crucial to its function in a moral argument. A recent writer, J. W. N. Watkins, has stated a similar view in advocating that moral principles be open to maximum criticism of their unsatisfactory implications and that it be not assumed, except in a closed moral system, that there are no unsatisfactory implications. He said:

> Rational discussion of moral principles consists, not in trying (hopelessly) to justify them, but in criticizing them; and this means, primarily, examining them for unsatisfactory implications.[22]

Finally, against the objection that acts of supererogation are thought to be E-type, the intention of their being praised is that they be approved, supported, emulated, and repeated. Hence they too are U-type. Universalizability, while open to denial in particular instances, is held to be a characteristic of a universal moral premise and thus a basis for assessing and criticizing moral premises in educational arguments.

The examination of unsatisfactory implications of the moral principle in M_2 leads to a consideration of the Instrumental Principle.

The Instrumental Principle

The universalizability of M_2 is a good reason for morally affirming it. Such a U-type principle is avoided in a Q_1 type of argument, which can begin with either M_1 or $\sim M_1$, according to preference, followed by I_1, to conclude with either T_1 or $\sim T_1$. The universalizability of M_2, on the contrary, counts as a good reason against beginning with $\sim M_2$. But the presence of M_2 does not of itself count as a good enough reason to affirm T_2 or to deny $\sim T_2$. The reasons follow.

There are all sorts of claimants to the title of universalizability. One can use M_2 but, by inserting I_2b in place of I_2, imply a conclusion that is incompatible with T_2, as follows (abbreviated Q_2b):

M_2 True accounts of the origin of human life on earth should be taught.

I_2b The Holy Scripture account of the origin of human life on earth is true.

T_2b Therefore, the Holy Scripture account of the origin of human life on earth should be (the one to be) taught.

Although universalizability provides a good reason for avoiding $\sim M_2$ in a Q_2 type of argument, one can always use M_2 and insert I_2b to imply validly T_2b. Hence, a U-type principle in M, although needed in order to avoid a $\sim Q_2$ type of argument, is not sufficient to avoid a Q_2b type of argument. After all, we only have a good enough reason for teaching certain subject matter if there is a good reason against beginning with $\sim$ M and also if there is a good enough reason to decide that we should act on T (and deny or reject $\sim$ T). This means we must have good reasons for premise I. There must be good reasons for all of the premises in the argument in order to have a *good enough* reason to accept T, a conclusion to which it would be logically odd to add, "But we shouldn't act on T." [23]

Premise I is empirically contingent and must, therefore, be true if it is to count as a good reason. Hence a Q-type of argument, in order to constitute a *good enough* reason, not only must have a universalizable moral premise but also must have a true, even though contingent, premise. If we had to withdraw I either in Q_2 or in Q_2b as a good reason for teaching certain subject matter, we would not have a good enough reason for deciding between T and $\sim$ T.

For a contingent premise I to be confirmable in experience, it must be capable of being falsified.[24] In Q_2, I_2 is falsifiable. If I_2b were said to be unfalsifiable, then it would have to be withdrawn as a good reason because it would not accord with the falsifiability condition of a Q type of argument. A fiat forbidding the withdrawal of an empirically contingent premise from the argument would militate against its assertibility as a good factual reason. For a factual proposition I to be assertible, it must not only be confirmed in experience but also must be capable of being falsified or refuted. Objection, for example, to the assertion that the earth does not move would rest not only on grounds that the assertion was false but also on grounds that it was regarded as unfalsifiable.

Although I is falsifiable, the argument, strictly speaking, is not. For, in choosing between T and ∼T, it would not do to speak of "falsifying" a conclusion that is not a factual assertion. T is a value judgment; it cannot, therefore, in a strict sense, be either confirmed or falsified.

Although a valuation like T cannot be asserted, it can be affirmed. A factual statement like I must be asserted, but can be asserted only if it can, in principle, be falsified; similarly, a value statement like T can be affirmed as bona fide only if it can, in principle, be denied or rejected as being wrong (not lightly, of course, but on analogous rational grounds). While asserting and affirming are different by virtue of what the speaker says in his proposition or decision, they are not so different as to exclude any logical similarity between what is asserted and what is affirmed. An assertion has meaning if there is a way to distinguish the conditions under which it is true or false; an affirmation has meaning if there is a way to distinguish the conditions under which it is right or wrong. Thus, just as a bona fide assertion is falsifiable, a bona fide value judgment is deniable or open to criticism; the deniability or criticizability of a value judgment (of the form T) is the evaluative counterpart of falsifiability.

The objectionable aspect to the way an evaluative argument is used to arrive at a conclusion of type T_2b is not its affirmation about a way of life but its insistence that it is undeniably right. What was an evaluative conclusion is eroded into one that is supported by appealing primarily to extrarational ordinances. If, for example, someone uses M_2 along with an unfalsifiable I to decide "A belief in X ought to be taught" (for any value of X), the test question is: "What counts against your affirmation that we should teach (for) a belief in X?" When, for example, someone affirms, "The teaching of atheism is morally wrong," the test questions are: "What would it take to deny your contention that the teaching of atheism is morally wrong? If there were no God, would it still be wrong? Is it wrong under any and all conditions?" (Note here the connection between metaphysics and morals, discussed in Chapter IV.) If the antiatheist denies that anything can dissuade him from what he believes, then he seems not to be making a rational appeal to a morally good reason for his contention that the teaching of atheism is wrong. When the believer (or, for that matter, the disbeliever) says that nothing can dissuade him from his belief, then he is using a fiat to rule out a conclusion of the form $\sim T$ (such as prohibiting the teaching of atheism), but he is not thereby giving us a good enough reason for prohibiting the teaching of a particular subject matter or for concluding against T. This may explain why metaphysical and theological arguments between atheists and theists are liable to break down: refusal by either or both to accept the conditions that would settle the argument.

Moreover, insistence by adherents to a T_2b type of affirmation that it cannot be denied does not mean that it cannot be denied on rational grounds. Undeniability here is merely the contention of believers that nothing can count against their affirmation. The difficulty is that while believers thus affirm with certainty that their belief is right, disbelievers find it possible to deny it with just as much conviction. There is no logical, and even sometimes no factual, impossibility of denying the affirmation of believers. A statement that is not permitted by its believers to be falsified may, in point of fact, even be shown to be false. Suppose, for example, that M_2, "True accounts of the origin of life on earth should be taught," were used in conjunction with I_2b, "The Holy Scripture is a true account of the origin of life on earth," as a presumably good enough reason for deciding to act on the conclusion T_2b, "The Holy Scripture should be taught (as giving the true account of the origin of life on earth)." Then, since the Holy Scripture is demonstrably a false account of the origin of life on earth, and a conjunction is true only if both its conjuncts are true, T_2b, the implied conclusion, could not be said to be true. Once it was established that the Holy Scripture is a false account of the origin of life on earth, I_2b would be falsified and consequently withdrawn as a good reason to act on the implied conclusion T_2b. (Otherwise, one would have to add the premise that falsehoods should be taught.) Since there is a good enough reason for a conclusion T only if the conjunction of premises taken together count as good reasons, the conclusion T_2b would have to be denied or rejected. Each of the premises in Q_2b must be a good reason, in order that the conjunction of premises taken together can provide a good enough reason for teaching certain subject matter. The falsification of I_2b—like unfalsifiability—would count against using it as a good reason for deciding to act on T_2b. This account may also take a step toward demonstrating how a metaphysical or theological world view or blik may be shown to depend indirectly and in part upon tacit factual assertions, a view very close to Flew's assertion-oriented view on bliks (see Chapter IV).

The Pedagogical Principle

Although M may be universalizable and I may be true (although falsifiable), it may not be logically odd to add, "But we shouldn't act on T?" Why one may still question acting on T has to do with the third condition for good enough reasons, relevance to teaching.

Even though M is U-type and I is true though falsifiable, acting on T—to teach certain subject matter—may nevertheless be irrelevant. T may not take into account the practice of teaching. There are some U-type values that seem highly desirable teach. Consider, for example, Q_4:

M_4 Children should be taught to make wise decisions.

I_4 Never drinking alcohol when driving is a wise decision.

T_4 Therefore, children should be taught never to drink alcohol while driving.[25]

There is nothing wrong with the argument: M_4 is U-type and I_4 is falsifiable. But can T_4 be taught? The difficulty of deciding whether what is proposed is teachable points up the rule of relevance, or the principle of pedagogy. In effect, this asks: Is there a method for teaching certain subject matter in such a way that it is learnable? M and I may be perfectly good reasons for deciding on a conclusion T but may not take into consideration the actual practice of teaching. Proposing that certain subject matter should be taught does not automatically mean that it can be taught. To say that it can be taught means (among other things) "taught meaningfully." To say that a lesson is "taught meaningfully," as that expression is understood in modern pedagogy, means that the lesson can be, through known teaching methods, successfully learned. The pedagogical rule of relevance attempts to guard against faulty or inadequate motivation, trivialization of instruction, and undue indoctrination.[26] The first and third factors are well enough known and so only trivialization is exemplified in Q_5 and Q_6:

M_5 The truth should be taught.

I_5 The truth is that red tulips grow in Holland.

T_5 Therefore, the fact that red tulips grow in Holland should be taught.

Or:

M_6 The truth should be taught.

I_6 The truth is that Plato ate his breakfast at 8:04 A.M. on his 50th birthday.

T_6 Therefore, the fact that Plato ate his breakfast at 8:04 A.M. on his 50th birthday should be taught.

To recall an earlier remark about "approval," the driving-drinking argument might be saved by our proposing that we teach people to *disapprove* of drinking while driving. Even this would be difficult, but it certainly would not seem possible without relevant attention to appropriate motivation, non-trivialization, and no undue indoctrination. (Note how the question of what to teach feeds into the question of how to teach).

Concerning the tulip and Plato examples, it can be imagined that in certain contexts the conclusions to teach that red tulips grow in Holland and that Plato ate his breakfast at 8:04 A.M. on his fiftieth birthday might seem important; but it can be more readily thought that such facts would make for dull or trivial teaching.

It is easier to designate what is trivial than what is significant, although recent studies of explanation and justification in scientific and moral philosophy are warrant against complete despair on the teaching of significant ideas.[27]

Applying the pedagogical condition as a good reason for deciding to act on teaching patriotism means that the proponent of that argument not only affirms the premise on attitudes and asserts the premise on national interest but also presupposes "Patriotism is learned by being taught"; or "If patriotism is taught in school, then it can be successfully learned." The pedagogical condition thus adds another empirically contingent assertion to considering whether the argument offers a good enough reason to decide to act on either the conclusion or its contradictory; it makes an assertion contingent on whether what is taught in school is in fact learned. Such a claim is especially difficult to maintain in connection with teaching attitudes and most especially in connection with teaching those exceptionally rate attitudes that "dedicated" teachers are said to have in mind. Exemplary moral learning is so seldom achieved as to be considered well-nigh unteachable. But the uncharacteristic virtues like those of the hero or saint, if learned, are thought to bring about such overwhelming human good and to diminish human ills so greatly that they are regarded as eminently worthy of emulation and come to be earmarked as universalizable. This is why, in relation to what it means to be moral, such attitudes with the highest moral rating are ideally *desiderated.* The desirability of teaching rare virtues leads to a question that is beyond the scope of this work: How do we test whether virtue can be taught? That is precisely what makes the pedagogical condition so difficult to follow; it says that if there is no method for teaching meaningfully, so that what is taught is learned, the pedagogical principle is unsatisfied. In the presence of the three-pronged considerations of relevance, the pedagogical principle is not easily satisfied.

Since the pedagogical condition, like the instrumental premise, is empirically contingent, it too is falsifiable; if P is falsified, we must withdraw the assumption that it is a good reason for deciding to act on T, for its falsification (*not* its falsifiability) would also count against the conclusion.

The pedagogical condition is not, strictly speaking, necessary in order for M and I logically to imply T. But if it is violated—if what shall be taught cannot be taught meaningfully or in principle learned successfully, so that we have ∼P—then a pedagogical condition for deciding to act on T is not fulfilled. Hence the falsification of the pedagogical condition counts as a good reason against deciding to act on T.[28]

If there is no method for teaching a subject matter meaningfully, the pedagogical principle is unsatisfied. If what is taught is only memorized and not genuinely learned, then it is pedagogically irrelevant.

Thus, even if M is universalizable and I contingently true, a good enough reason for choosing to act on T may still be lacking if the pedagogical principle is either used unfalsifiably, by not functioning as an empirical rule of relevance, or else is falsified.

Note that a good enough reason is one that helps us to "act on" one conclusion rather than another. An argument may be perfectly valid, M may be universalizable and I may be true; but if there is no *method* for teaching a certain subject matter meaningfully, then the rule of relevance is unsatisfied. If something that is taught is not genuinely learned but is indoctrinated or memorized, then it is pedagogically irrelevant. If a proposal is made that we should teach a certain subject matter, yet takes no account of the conditions of learning and the practice of teaching, then the proposal, for all that it may be perfectly valid, perfectly moral, and perfectly true, may also be perfectly irrelevant. (The kind of moral platitude noted in Q_4 or Q_5 may, without further pedagogical considerations, be precisely of the kind that fails to satisfy the pedagogical rule of relevance.)

The Use of a Good Enough Reason for Deciding What Shall Be Taught

A Q type of argument gives a good enough reason for deciding to act on one of two contradictory answers to the question "What shall be taught?" if there is a universalizable moral principle, and if the answer is open to denial through the falsifiability of the instrumental premise and relevant pedagogical considerations. The rule of relevance, in particular, commits the proponent of a T-type conclusion to draw upon counterarguments against it, and to show under what conditions in the instrumental or pedagogical premises he would withdraw his proposal for acting on T. The welter of objections that a Q_2 type of argument withstands helps to furnish its choice-guiding function and enables us to say that in Q_2 we have a good enough reason for choosing between T_2 and

$\sim T_2$–a conclusion to which it would then be logically odd to add: "But we shouldn't act on it."

There is a sense in which we can use the openness to falsification of both the instrumental and relevance assertions to check, albeit indirectly, on whether M performs the job of a genuine U-type principle (affording a basis for denial and rejection, if it does not.) Whether M is particular or universal depends on how its terms such as "national interest" or "truth" are used: we get a significant clue as to how M is used by observing with what other premises it is joined. We get an idea of how the expression "true statement" is used by looking at I. In I_2b_5, "true statement" is used as part of an unfalsifiable sentence. We test the expressions in M, albeit indirectly, by seeing how they are used in I. The terms in the argument must be used in the same way throughout the argument. The use of M is indirectly tested by whether the argument as a whole is open or closed to rational criticism of its unsatisfactory implications. To the extent that it is open or closed, the argument as a whole gains or loses application. An argument that is, as a whole, empty and bereft of application, because its unsatisfactory implications are not permitted to be criticized, endangers M with erosion into a worn-out platitude. Although we may pay lip service to it, M no longer does its job of distinguishing sharply between what should and should not be taught. A Q-type of argument gains in application to the extent that M can be taken in conjunction with another true premise and a pedagogical consideration, both of which are open to pertinent forms of rational criticism of their unsatisfactory implications.

The openness of the argument as a whole to the foregoing criticism enables M to be used to inveigh against nearly undetectable and infrequently exhibited non–U-type principles that sometimes filter into the moral language of education.

If M is sharpened in this way, we then endow our keenest moral perceptions with the power to guide our choice of what shall be taught.

By way of synopis and conclusion, let it be repeated that the presence of M and I, although necessary to imply T in a valid argument, is not a *good enough* reason for deciding to act on either of two contradictory alternatives—T or $\sim$T. Needed are good reasons to imply T and also a good enough reason for deciding that we should act on T and reject $\sim$T. A good enough reason consists of a valid, non-empty argument with premises that are backed by good reasons to furnish, in turn, a good reason for believing in the conclusion, and, if pedagogically relevant, to furnish a good reason to decide to act on T rather than $\sim$T.[29]

A good enough reason for teaching a certain subject matter would, then, imply a conclusion to which it would be logically odd to add, "But we shouldn't teach that." But what counts as a good enough reason to guide our choice between two contradictory alternatives? The example of Q_2 gives, or comes close to giving, an example of a good enough reason to decide between T_2 and $\sim T_2$; this is in contrast to both Q_1 and Q_2b, although in each case on different grounds. In Q_1, instead of starting with M_1, one can begin with $\sim$M and, by combining it with I_1 (assuming relevancy to be true) decide not to act on T_1. Not so with Q_2, because M_2 is universalizable and a U-type principle counts as a good reason against denying M_2. But one can also use M_2 along with I_2b to imply T_2b, which is logically incompatible with T_2. Although a U-type principle is necessary against a Q_1 argument, it does not work against a Q_2b argument. A U-type principle, though it counts as a *good reason to act on T*, is not by itself *a good enough reason to decide between T and $\sim$T*. As was noted, additional reasons are needed, such as I, a contingent premise, and the empirical rule of relevance to test whether what is taught is learned. The test of empirical assertibility is the falsifiability of both I and relevance, and the openness to criticism of the argument as a whole. (The importance of having a way to criticize rationally an evaluative conclusion of the form T is understood if in teaching values of any stripe we allow, in Isaiah Berlin's phrase, final ends of life to collide.)

In Q_2b, I_2b is unfalsifiable. So Q_2b does not count as a good enough reason to choose T_2b over $\sim T_2b$. While a moral principle, taken together with other good reasons, guides our choice of what to teach, the absence of these good reasons for acting on a T-type conclusion can be used to rebut the decision to act on T.

In an argument that is closed to criticism, M fails to function as a U-type principle. (This is the point at which to mention the salutary effect of the Instrumentalist position noted in Chapter III, for it inveighs against closed moral systems and against such arguments as Q_2b, in which I_2b is not permitted to be falsified. According to the Instrumentalist means-end notion, a valuation like M_2 means no more than its relation to other statements in the argument.) Once an argument is closed to criticism, it becomes empty and bereft of application; soon M deteriorates into a mere platitude.[30] M is then not doing its job of inveighing against non–U-type principles in the moral language of education and hence is not assisting our moral perceptions to guide our choice of what should be taught.[31] (This may also explain what is objectionable about the traditional metaphysical approach in education, as noted in Chapters III and IV: these isms are not open to criticism of their unsatisfactory implications.)

Does the question "What should be taught?" have an answering argument that resembles Sense II? It seems to have such an argument when we have a good enough reason to decide between two contradictory conclusions that purportedly answer the question. What is needed is a good enough reason to decide between alternative arguments.

But even though good reasons, difficult as they are to find, are available, a good enough reason is in practice well-nigh unobtainable. Some comfort might come from asking why, in Zeno's paradox, the hare keeps chasing the tortoise that he cannot catch. At any rate, when next we encounter an answer to the question "What should be taught?", we might ask how that answer follows from the reasons given in its defense. By this simple mode we are apt to see that what we are told should be taught does not always follow from the reasons given—or, if it does, so does its contradictory.

If, in the face of genuine difficulties, we do not care to seek a good enough reason for deciding what to teach, there may be no serious harm in it. Perhaps we shall then all go about our various ways saying, "We have an argument to answer the question 'What shall be taught?' "; and undoubtedly, we shall have an argument—only it will have to be written within inverted commas (like sense I).

Other conditions for assessing the use of moral arguments in education are undoubtedly needed. In defense of the view that moral reasons do apply to evaluative arguments in education, this study has tried to show how several canons of criticism may be used to assess one conclusion of the form T. The conclusion may come close to being backed by a good enough reason, so that it can rationally be chosen over some alternative conclusion of the form T that is not nearly as well backed by good reasons.

Evaluative arguments in education may still go on being treated, on the one hand, like "I like peach pie," indiscernibly hortatory, or, on the other hand, like a quest for a philosopher's stone,[32] indiscriminable or inapplicable; neither treatment provides rational canons of criticism suitable to the assessment of evaluative arguments in education. A view that there is no way out of the impasse between Sense I and Sense II, between the Capricious and the Purist, may become buttressed by the notion that there is "nothing good or bad, but thinking makes it so." Is it any wonder that under such auspices, old or new, virtue cannot be taught?

1. See, for example, B. Othanel Smith, "Views on the Role of Philosophy in Teacher Education."

2. See, for example, *Moral and Spiritual Values in the Public Schools* (Washington, D.C.: National Education Association, 1951).

3. J. J. C. Smart, *Philosophy and Scientific Realism* (New York: Humanities Press, 1963), p. 3.

4. In this connection, see Paul Taylor, *Normative Discourse* (Englewood Cliffs, N.J.: Prentice-Hall, 1961), chap. vi.

5. "Patriotism" is used here the way John Dixon uses it in C. Winfield Scott and Clyde M. Hill (eds.), *Public Education under Criticism* (Englewood Cliffs, N.J.: Prentice-Hall, 1954). The "patriots" believe in "My country, right or wrong."

If I_1 is a particular premise, then T would be a particular conclusion, which would raise the difficulty brought about by the fact that Frankena's MEM's (chap. iv) yield a particular conclusion. If the conclusion is particular, then each group can teach its values to its members (e.g., Lutherans, Thomists, Idealists, Experimentalists), but they have decided nothing between them as to what should be taught *at large.*

If one starts off with a particular premise but thereupon draws a universal conclusion, then there is more in the conclusion than there was in the premises. Hence, the Q form of argument here used assumes that the premises and conclusion are both universal, an assumption I argue for in Section 3 of this chapter.

6. The contingent premise is not, however, particular. If premise I is particular, not only does the conclusion have to be particular; but, while it is possible to verify an I proposition, it is not possible to falsify it. Only a universal proposition can be falsified. See J. Urmson, *Philosophical Analysis* (Oxford: Clarendon Press, 1956), p. 113, for this difficulty in Popper's account.

7. *The Language of Morals,* p. 28. According to this rule, "is" is not synonymous with "ought." If "is" meant the same thing as "ought," it would be self-contradictory to say "X is the case, but X ought not to be the case." One could then not take exception to what was the case and yet ought not to be the case. One could then argue from "Hitler killed six million Jews" to "See, that proves it's right." Or one could point to some instance of segregated schooling, and say "That proves it's right" (see Chapter III).

8. Therein too lies the difficulty that arises if one confuses logical implications with justification, which seemed to be the case with some philosophers of education discussed in Chapter II, and also with Frankena's MEM's discussed in Chapter IV. The reason I boggle in the case of Q_1 being used as if it were not only valid but justified is that (a) validity is not justification (which may also explain the Purist-Capricious impasse in Chapter I) and (b) for forthcoming reasons I shall maintain that Q_1 is, though valid, not justified.

9. The argument here is set up to take into account Frankena's MEM's in as much as his MEM's can be used for either the metaphysical or moral argument.

Note, too, that I_2 assumes a general empiricist or materialist world view that appeals to scientific facts for the paradigmatic use of "true.'" Hence, the relation of metaphysics to morals, epistemology, and education, which cannot but be (tacitly) involved in deciding whether to teach biological evolution or not.

10. See Chapter IV for an elaboration of the use of factual assertions in conjunction with MEM's to back evaluative conclusions, and especially the criticism there of Paley's metaphor or blik.

11. Morris R. Cohen and Ernest Nagel, *An Introduction to Logic and Scientific Method* (New York: Harcourt Brace, 1934), p. 80. If the conclusion is regarded as particular, and I is a particular contingent premise, then M would have had to be universal, because of the theorem that states, "If both premises are particular, there is no conclusion." But a particular premise cannot be used to imply a universal conclusion, and if T is universal, then both M and I have to be universal. The chief difficulty with Frankena's MEM arguments, as suggested in Chapter IV, consists in the particularity of the conclusions (e.g., Teach a Judeo-Christian conception of God *in non-public, sectarian schools*). The main educational difficulty discussed in Chapters I, II, and III seemed to be the attempt to draw a universal conclusion from particular premises. Frankena's MEM's do not overcome this difficulty.

If the conclusion is universal, the premises must be universal. Also, if premise I were particular, it would be verifiable but not falsifiable. If I were universal and M particular, then the conclusion would again be particular. For T to be universal, M and I must therefore both be universal.

The reason this rule refers not only to logical validity is that there is no logical requirement to have a universal conclusion, but it is, it will be argued here, a necessary condition of the kind of evaluative argument in education in which one wants to know how one ought to decide between opposing arguments.

12. Thomas Kingsmill Abbot (ed.), *Kant's Critique of Practical Reason and Other Works on the Theory of Ethics* (6th ed.; London: Longman's, 1909), p. 47.

13. *Ibid.*, p. 47.

14. E. A. Gellner, "Ethics and Logic," in *Proceedings of the Aristotelian Society*, New Series, LV (London: Harrison & Sons, 1955), 157–78.

15. Richard M. Hare, "Universalizability," *ibid.*, pp. 295–312.

16. If, for the limited purpose of trying to detect universalizability, M is reformulated to read, "We should teach . . . X," one can then look to the scope and limits of "we." There are, it seems, two main uses of "we" in education. There is, first, the use of "we" to express partisan *assent* to, or *advocacy* of, an educational point of view or ism (see Chapters II and III for some similar instances in metaphysical and moral arguments). There is, second, the use of "we" to express *allegiance* or *consent* to vaguely formulated ideals, as in "We hold these truths to be self-evident. . . . " and "We, the people. . . . " The former is somewhat like the advocate's use of "we"; the latter is somewhat like the verdict-giving use of "we." (This distinction bears similarity to the two senses of argument noted in Chapter I.) On occasion, a "we" sentence in one sense will shift almost imperceptibly into another sense. See, for example, J. Dixon, "What's Wrong with U.S. History?" in Scott and Hill (eds.), *Public Education under Criticism*, p. 153; also Arthur Eugene Bestor, *Educational Wastelands: The Retreat from Learning in Our Public Schools* (Urbana: University of Illinois Press, 1953); and *Moral and Spiritual Values in the Public Schools*, pp. 33–34. For a philosophical consideration of "we" sentences, see M. B. Foster, " 'We' in Modern Philosophy," in Basil Mitchell (ed.), *Faith and Logic* (London; Allen & Unwin, 1957), pp. 210–19.

One reason, however, for looking to singularity in terms other than "we" in a value-implying syllogism is that, if M is reformulated, using "We" in M as well as in the conclusion, the syllogism is invalid, because the middle term is undistributed:

M_1 We should teach attitudes that serve the national interest.

I_1 Patriotism (is an attitude that) serves the national interest.

T_1 Therefore, we should teach patriotism.

I am indebted to two former colleagues: to Professor Arnold Berleant, for pointing out a difficulty that occurs when using "we," namely, that the middle term is undistributed; and to Professor Joseph La Lumia for suggesting the alternative formulation whereby the middle term is distributed.

The reason is that in a BARBARA figure, the A proposition does not distribute its predicate, and a rule of the syllogism says that the middle term must be distributed in the premises at least once. In using the "we" formulation above, the middle term "national interest" is undistributed.

Bearing the above qualifications in mind, there are some advantages to considering M as a "we" sentence—namely, that "we" in "We should teach X" focuses upon the intentional and performative aspects of teaching. In the first person plural, as with the first person singular ("I know" or "I do"), commitment is expressed; although in the plural, allegiance is pluralized, and alludes to those doing the teaching—namely, the profession of teachers—rather than to other groups who purport to decide what to teach. Because there are so many difficulties with the use of "we," moral and otherwise, which have not even been touched on, M is here used as it appears in the argument in the body of this work.

17. It is ordinarily an anomaly to prescribe that falsehoods be taught, for the idea of teaching falsehood, if universalized, would generally be self-defeating.

18. John Hospers, *Human Conduct: An Introduction to the Problems* (New York: Harcourt Brace, 1961), p. 572.

19. This ingenious example was originally suggested by Professor Philip Phenix.

20. J. O. Urmson, "Saints and Heroes," in Abraham I. Melden (ed.), *Essays in Moral Philosophy* (Seattle: University of Washington Press, 1958), pp. 198–216.

21. Gilbert Ryle, "On Forgetting the Difference between Right and Wrong," *ibid.*, p. 159.

22. J. W. N. Watkins, "Negative Utilitarianism," *Proceedings of the Aristotelian Society,* Supplementary Volume, XXXVIII (London: Harrison & Sons, 1963), 108.

23. This represents an effort to remedy, in part, the deficiency in Frankena's treatment of MEM's of not specifying what count as good reasons for all the premises.

24. For a detailed discussion of falsifiability, see Karl Popper, "Philosophy of Science: A Personal Report," in C. A. Mace (ed.), *British Philosophy in Mid-Century* (New York: Macmillan, 1957), pp. 155–56.

25. The desirability of teaching children to make wise decisions is suggested by Woodring in *One Fourth of a Nation,* p. 111. He says, "In a society of free men, the proper aim of education is to prepare the individual to make wise decisions. All else is but contributory." Teaching children to make wise decisions is assuredly a laudable aim, but the pedagogical rule reminds us that a lofty aim does not mean very much if no method is available for assuring that what is taught is learned. If one may here echo Kant, means without ends are blind, and ends without means are empty. The concern with making ends meaningful by showing that they are to be considered in relation to means, is a lesson learned from a study of the Instrumentalist approach (see Chapter III).

26. I use "undue" because I do not wish to propose a definition of teaching that goes counter to common usage; and it does seem, opponents of indoctrination notwithstanding, that teaching has had three sometimes related usages: (a) indoctrinating or inducting the young in the sense of socializing them; (b) citing facts, definitions, explanations, and formulas; and (c) questioning, doubting, examining, and criticizing prevailing beliefs, attitudes, and facts. I use the word "undue" because some societies and groups do seem to stress *a* and *b* at the expense of *c*, and the argument is that they thereby go counter to common usage. The same argument applies to those who, like Scheffler, define teaching mainly as *c*; teaching, it seems, also includes socializing and to this end even indoctrination, but not unduly. See Scheffler, *The Language of Education,* p. 57, for a persuasive definition of teaching that emphasizes *c*, although it seems that *a* and *b* also fall into the standard range of the term "teaching."

27. See, for example, in this connection, Scheffler, "Justifying Curriculum Decisions," pp. 461–72, for an elucidation of what he there and in *The Language of Education,* p. 90, calls "the generalization

requirement." See also Jane Roland Martin, "The Historian as Teacher," *Philosophy of Education Proceedings,* 1962, and her criticism of Bantok in the Fall, 1963 issue of the *Harvard Educational Review,* "Can There Be Universally Applicable Criteria of Good Teaching?" pp. 484–90.

28. For a more detailed discussion of P, see McClellan, "Why Should the Humanities Be Taught?", p. 1005; also B. Othanel Smith, "The Concept of Teaching," in Smith and Ennis (eds.), *Language and Concepts in Education;* and Scheffler, *The Language of Education,* chap. ii.

29. This may well be the point to remark that the initial dissatisfaction with the Purist use of argument as presented, for example, by Smullyan in Chapter I, is not, as Toulmin held, that the logician's ideal is too abstract but, rather, that its rules and modes of rational criticism are *insufficient* adequately to criticize unsatisfactory implications of evaluative arguments in education.

30. Q gains or loses application depending on whether or not it can be rationally criticized, i.e., whether or not it is open to maximum criticism of its unsatisfactory implications; and if it is not, then M, even though it is "universalizable," likewise withers.

31. It is not, however, a moral principle alone that helps us to decide what to teach. It is the moral principle taken together with other good reasons, metaphysical and epistemological (see Chapter IV), as well as factual and pedagogical ones, that guide our choice of what to teach. The absence of either of these reasons for acting on a T-type conclusion can be used to criticize and even rebut the decision that T ought to be acted on.

32. See McClellan, "Dewey and the Concept of Method: Quest for the Philosopher's Stone in Education."

VI. *The Rebuttal Notion*

The difficulty that has been noted in philosophy of education is the absence of rational canons of criticism by which to assess philosophical arguments in education. This lack permits the existence of a situation in which someone concludes a given argument with X, while someone else concludes the same argument with $\sim X$ or Y. Which is right? How does one assess the arguments? An outstanding illustration of this difficulty is the type of argument used in philosophy of education to answer Spencer's question, "What knowledge is of most worth?" An answer is used as a *response*, in Sense I, and then is treated as if it were a *solution*, in Sense II. This often nearly imperceptible shift from Sense I, response, to Sense II, solution, is "of the last consequence"; nevertheless, it occurs in philosophy even more generally than in philosophy of education.

The attempt to apply canons of criticism from mathematics or science, however, does not seem to be a useful way to assess educational arguments because the rules and strictures in these terms are too restrictive to apply to the criticism of educational arguments. The logician's idealized model of argument has been called here the Purist use of argument, and the whimsical kind of argument often used in philosophy of education has been termed Capricious.

It would be fine if criteria did exist to help us assess educational arguments in order to distinguish between those arguments one ought to heed and those one should ignore or rebut. No criteria, however, seem suitable. In the absence of formalized canons of criticism, we may have to live with the preliminary step—uncovering the difficulties that lie in the way of rationally criticizing educational arguments that purport to answer the question "What should be taught?" An argument in Sense I is like a debate or quarrel;[1] in Sense II it is like a formal proof.[2] The difficulty with Sense I is that the use of argument in education is not readily open to criticism, and hence there has arisen a "democracy" among arguments in which anything goes. The difficulty with Sense II is that there are no criteria for criticizing evaluative arguments or proving conclusions that purport to answer a question like Spencer's. An argument in Sense II is valid, sound, and rigorous (Smullyan); to be rigorous it must be "correctly annotated." The Purist ideal furnishes a purely univocal standard for criticizing and assessing arguments.

We have considered Toulmin's appeal to the use of ordinary arguments in various working contexts, emphasizing the jurisprudential context. We found this to be helpful but too unrestrictive. One obtains a verdict in a law court; but is it necessarily true or right? How does one assess educational arguments?

A main difficulty seems to be that arguments that begin by being used in Sense I sometimes slide into Sense II and are suddenly made to look as if they were proofs. Hume expressed concern with a similar shift from "is" to "ought," which he found also to be "of the last consequence." Abraham Kaplan's lead in distinguishing among ethical theories has been followed in terming Sense I and its tendency to shift to another sense the Capricious use of argument. We find many examples of this phenomenon in philosophy of education (as noted in Chapters I, II, and III). Opposed to the Capricious use is the strict use of argument in Sense II—as a formal proof or empirical confirmation—and this has been termed here the Purist use of the word argument.

The questions are these: Are there any rational canons of criticism that can be used to evaluate educational arguments? How, in particular, does one answer Spencer's question in a way that is more like Sense II than Sense I? Or is Spencer's question to be answered in the same way that one answers the question "How do you feel about Communism?" If there are no rational canons of criticism by which to assess evaluative arguments in education, then the use of arguments in Sense I strengthens the view that ours is an Alice-in-Wonderland sort of world, in which any argument will do as well as any other. Yet an argument intended in Sense II fails if, among logically incompatible alternatives, there is no way to decide which one is right, or at least which one can be criticized. The result is that we either have too many arguments, none of which is intended as a valid, sound, and rigorous proof, or else we have at least two logically incompatible arguments, both of which are intended as proofs—with no way to choose between them. That is the dilemma of the philosophical argument in education, which has been called here the Purist-Capricious impasse.

How metaphysical and moral arguments are used in education was considered in order to ascertain in detail the nature of the difficulty of assessing educational arguments. It was noted that these arguments are intended to be demonstrated, and their conclusions not only implied but also justified. A difficulty in each instance was that more appeared in the conclusion than there was in the premises. A metaphysical argument, in particular, consisting of a definition or belief, was concluded in Sense I, although Sense II was clearly intended.

Consideration was given next to three prominent efforts to use moral arguments. These, too, were not used in such a way as to put Spencer's question to rest. Was there no way out of the Purist-Capricious impasse?

Summary of Attempted Solution

A suggested way out was Frankena's notion of MEM's (metaphysical, epistemological, and metamoral premises). Frankena argued that some MEM's were relevant and even necessary, although not sufficient, to imply and even justify some educational conclusions. His method was not as helpful, however, as his format; for we were still left with the dilemma of not knowing which MEM to choose—between, for example, one that says there is a God and one that says there is not. Frankena did not succeed in showing how to assess and criticize MEM's.

It was observed that metaphysical premises in education are sometimes expressed as "root metaphors" or pictures depicting man, society, and the universe in ideal terms. Noted, also, was how Scheffler's two modes of criticism could be applied to educational metaphors. According to Scheffler, analogies can be criticized for being trivial, and they can be shown to be limited or to break down in their application.[3]

The discussion of metaphors was extended to involve "bliks," metaphors writ large, more like the "root metaphors" that Othanel Smith discussed than the epistemologically-oriented metaphors that Scheffler discussed. The problem Frankena had left with us was whether or not there is a God, which was also a problem of the fundamental kind noted in Chapter I. It was argued that root metaphors or bliks, by encompassing the relations of man, society, the universe, and God, were open to the type of analogical criticism suggested by Scheffler. This was illustrated by Paley's metaphor and by a board of education policy statement; in applying Hume's analogical arguments to Paley's metaphor, some criticisms were made of this kind of world view. The educational policy statement revealed a direct relationship between metaphysics and what is taught; and the possibility of criticizing the metaphor or blik seemed to take a step toward showing that metaphysics is not necessarily irrelevant to education.

The possibility of criticizing metaphysical premises, although helpful, was not, however, regarded as sufficient to decide between contradictory educational conclusions. There was also needed a rational basis for criticizing and assessing moral premises and the relevant factual and pedagogical considerations that are used to support one educational conclusion as against another. It was maintained that an evaluative argument performs a choice-guiding function if it provides a good enough reason for deciding that one conclusion to teach certain subject matter should be acted on rather than another. But what counts as a good enough reason, so that it would become logically odd to say, "But we shouldn't teach that subject matter"?

Three considerations were proposed as what counts: universalizability in the major premise; falsifiability in the minor premise; and a pedagogical principle in criticizing and assessing the conclusion. These were proposed for application to the argument if it were to provide a good enough reason to decide that one conclusion of form T ("Teach X") should be acted on as against another.

This proposal does not result in a proof, pure and simple, but it is hoped that it may be something to reckon with. An argument, accordingly, need not be merely a futile quarrel or debate, nor need it be a sterile proof or demonstration. An argument may also consist (as Webster's Dictionary suggests) of a set of reasons for or against some contention, and this may provide a way out of the Purist-Capricious impasse.

Thus, an evaluative argument in education may be used as a quarrel or debate, or as proof or demonstration, or as a set of reasons for or against some contention. The difficulty with the first—a quarrel—is that there is in education often no rational way to criticize or assess it, much less settle it. The trouble with the second is that there are no proofs for criticizing or assessing difficult evaluative arguments that purport to answer the question "What should be taught?" The third use of argument, which gives reasons for or against a conclusion, may provide a way out of the Purist-Capricious impasse. This may be referred to as the third sense of an argument or Sense III. While not rigorous or strict, an argument in Sense III may be thought of as "cogent." A cogent argument is defined as one that is compelling, convincing, or telling to the mind or reason.[4]

A cogent argument is not as strict or rigorous as the kind Smullyan describes, for it offers no airtight proof. It may be that we cannot hope for a wholly rigorous argument in education or even for one that is conclusive and not open to rebuttal. It may be enough that a cogent argument, in appealing to reason, is a telling argument, a strong enough one to rebut an opposing, less cogent argument. (Cogency, unlike rigor, is a matter of degree.)

Calling educational arguments cogent does not make them so; it still remains to be shown whether, in fact, they are. In this connection it would seem a gross anomaly to suggest that the premises of an argument might furnish a good enough reason for deciding what to teach and at the same time be not compelling to the mind and convincing or, in short, cogent. It does not, accordingly, seem an untoward strain of language to suggest that an argument that is backed by a good enough reason is by that very fact a cogent argument.

This third sense of an argument need be neither rigorous nor capricious. An argument is identified by some writers as giving reasons of the sort Scheffler meant when he spoke of an "ordered argument" to support a decision concerning what to teach,[5] and which James McClellan further specified as follows:

> . . . "Why should the humanities be taught?" requires an argument for its answer, a set of premises . . . in such manner that they consititute good reasons for assenting to "The humanities should be taught." [6]

We cannot hope for a wholly rigorous argument, but a cogent argument will do as well for our purposes. It may not be conclusive, but it is to be hoped that it will appeal to reason as a telling argument that puts adversaries on notice that now it is their move. It has this proviso—such an argument must be open to the maximum criticism of its own unsatisfactory implications. We can—and it is contended that this is a way out of the Purist-Capricious impasse—offer reasons for or against, as well as for and against, our conclusions.

The lack of rigor and the readiness to give rigor up for cogency in an educational argument may not be completely regrettable, if one remembers Aristotle's observation:

> Our discussion will be adequate if it has as much clearness as the subject matter admits of, for precision is not to be sought for alike in all discussions. . . . And we must . . . not look for precision in all things alike, but in each class of things such precision as accords with the subject matter, and so much as is appropriate to the inquiry. For a carpenter and a geometer investigate the right angles in different ways; the former does so in so far as the right angle is useful for his work, while the latter inquires what it is or what sort of thing it is; for he is a spectator of the truth.[7]

Because a cogent argument is not rigorous, it may be said to be "non-cognitive" and therefore to fail to satisfy Sense II; but what is wrong with an evaluative argument, if it is *nearly* cognitive? It may at least be more like Sense II than Sense I, although if one prefers a rigorous argument for deciding what should be taught, one can always wait for Godot.

As to the central problem of this study, what, if anything, counts as a rational argument to answer the question "What should be taught?", there may be a solution other than the Purist and the Capricious uses of the word "argument." This solution would be a good enough reason with a requisite degree of conclusiveness to help us decide between two contradictory conclusions, both of which purportedly answer an evaluative question such as, "What knowledge is of most worth?" or, "What should be taught?" In the effort to criticize and assess evaluative arguments in education, the attempt was made to show that a good enough reason would count as a cogent argument in defense of an evaluative conclusion in education.

The rub is that a good enough reason may in practice be nearly unobtainable. Attempting to cite a cogent argument in order satisfactorily to answer Spencer's question (in Sense III or like Sense II) may very well be like the hare attempting to catch the tortoise or the geometer attempting to square the circle. If, however, the effort to show that there is a place for cogent evaluative arguments in education is likewise doomed, that is to say, is impossible or interminable or undecidable, that has yet to be demonstrated. In this study an attempt has been made to show that a good enough reason counts as a cogent evaluative argument in education and that, therefore, the effort to answer Spencer's question and the effort to use an argument to answer the question "What should be taught?" need not be doomed to a counsel of despair and need not be judged futile or interminable.

The Rebuttal Notion

Although it has been argued here that there are no strict proofs in evaluative arguments, the reader should not be left empty-handed. There is a limited sense in which an evaluative argument, such as that used to answer the question "What should be taught?", may be rebutted. If an evaluative argument in education is intended to be concluded in Sense II and is then shown not to be concluded in that sense but in a way very much more like Sense I (capriciously), we would have a reason to rebut that use of such an argument.

We do not say to Spencer and McGucken, "Stop arguing as to what knowledge is of most worth." We say, "If you intend to use an argument strictly in Sense II, as with an argument purporting to decide what should be taught, and expect a conclusion that is like Sense II, but without mustering up a good enough reason for choosing one conclusion over another, then your argument gives a reason for rebuttal." The absence of a good enough reason for deciding to act on one or another conclusion is a reason to rebut the argument—but only, it should be added, in the limited sense that the argument, which was intended to be concluded in Sense II, has been shown instead to have been concluded on grounds that more nearly resemble Sense I.[8]

An argument is rebuttable when its conclusion seems like an ironclad Sense II but its backing, proving on inspection to be flimsy, actually produces a conclusion more like Sense I. In taking on an aspect for which it has no backing or credentials, this use of argument has undergone an imperceptible shift, which it seemed suitable to call *capricious*. The use of an argument is to be rebutted, in short, when it appears like Sense II but is really more like Sense I. Even this limited rebuttal notion may show the difference between a flimsy argument, which is more like Sense I, and a cogent argument, which is more nearly like Sense II than Sense I.

The rebuttal of an evaluative argument does not, however, banish all its uses in education, nor does it make an argument that fails at one time to measure up as cogent (backed by a good enough reason) an argument that is forever wrong. The observed absence of a good enough reason does not mean that the deficiency cannot be remedied; it is logically possible for the rebutted conclusion to turn out to be the right one after all, if overriding reasons arise (see Chapter V), and this possibility cannot be ignored in evaluative arguments. Good reasons and even reasons that for a time are good enough do not accordingly stamp an argument as conclusive in the same sense as proofs do. (A good enough reason is the halfway station between proof and caprice.)

The rebuttal notion is therefore also limited by the possibility of giving a good enough reason to a conclusion where formerly there was none. Rebuttal constitutes only a form of criticism, and as such it is not infallible. Neither, however, is imperviousness to criticism. Indeed, one earmark of an evaluative argument, for which analogous work was begun by Karl Popper's work on falsification, is that an open evaluative (or philosophical) argument, whether theological, metaphysical, moral, esthetic, or educational, is open to rebuttal. This means that rebuttal conditions accompany a proposed argument in such a way that in the language game of arguing, the rules of that game show what counts as a "checkmate" (akin to the deniability notion set forth in the preceding chapter.)

Concluding Remarks

One may still ask: "What is a rational argument? Is it one that rules out metaphysical or moral premises?"

A rational argument need not be one that rules out metaphysical or moral premises. There are too many instances of rigorous arguments with successfully proven conclusions that are exceedingly dull and quite irrelevant to the problems of life; and we probably all know other arguments on tenuous, even shaky premises—hypotheses, principles, Ideas or Forms (as Plato called them)—purporting to answer questions such as, "How ought we to live?" or, "What is the world made of?" that may not successfully answer the questions, but seem to be both interesting and important. Arguments that attempt to answer these questions may for a time appear unsubstantiated, even implausible. Some rigorous arguments may demonstrate extremely trivial conclusions, while some less substantial arguments may provide the flimsiest sort of support for a significant conclusion.

The hesitation to rule out metaphysical and moral premises in an educational argument may be best explained by emphasizing something said earlier: One cannot be sure that the sort of metaphysical views put forward by Thales, Anaximander, Plato, and the early Greeks may not be ultimately the most important kinds of thoughts in the power of the mind of man to conceive. It should now be added that, for the education of man, it is doubtful that the idea of the Moral Law—with appropriate built-in qualifications—is very much less important. Yet, as premises, neither metaphysical nor moral arguments are capable of certain proof. Other arguments abound that are rigorous and thus rational, but they are also trivial in that they have no appreciable bearing on deciding what one ought to teach—that is, how one ought to teach the young to live.

In the effort to assess what counts as a rational argument in education, therefore, metaphysical and moral premises have not all been ruled in, nor have they all been ruled out. Instead, the attempt in this study has been to do two things: to apply rational canons of criticism toward assessing metaphysical and moral arguments in education; and, in this connection, to stress maximum criticizability of unsatisfactory metaphysical and moral implications. As J. W. N. Watkins suggests, this activity seems allied with doing the critical part of philosophy; the synoptic or visionary part, perhaps the more precious and difficult to come by, remains largely and regrettably untouched here.

The job of clearing the ground a little does not permit the luxury of constructing an airtight proof, or of judging either a metaphysical or moral argument in education once and for all. The job of quarrying for a cogent evaluative argument in education is intended to provide us with the power to criticize and assess what ought to be taught, with a view to preventing some harm that might otherwise be done.

1. See, for example, a chapter entitled "A Quarrel Among Educators," in Conant, *The Education of American Teachers.*

2. See, for example, Smullyan, *Fundamentals of Logic.*

3. Scheffler, *The Language of Education,* p. 48.

4. See *Webster's Collegiate Dictionary,* p. 195.

5. "Justifying Curriculum Decisions," p. 461.

6. Why Should the Humanities Be Taught?", p. 998.

7. Richard R. McKeon (ed.), *The Basic Works of Aristotle* (New York: Random House, 1941), 1094b and 1098b.

The effort here has been to follow Toulmin's advice that "We must judge each field of substantial arguments by its own relevant standards" and that we ought to be "demanding of arguments not that they shall measure up against analytic standards, but . . . that they shall achieve whatever sort of cogency or well-foundedness can relevantly be asked for in that field." S. Toulmin, *Uses of Argument,* pp. 234 and 248.

8. In this connection, see K. Popper, "The Pre-Socratics," *Proceedings of the Aristotelian Society,* 1962.

Index

Index

"Acceptable" premises, 103–4, 107–8
"Achievement" words, 31
Adler, Mortimer J., 46, 76–78
Analogy: and analogical argument, 122; and analogical criticism, 182; suggested by metaphor, 111; testing of, 111–12, 122; *see also* Metaphors
Analysans, 113
Anscombe, G., 87 n. 10
Answer, 26, 33; Capricious use of, 35–37; evaluative, 28; factual, 28, 33; formal, 28, 33; intentional use of, 30, 31; Purist use of, 35–37, 87; in Sense I, 27–33, 44; in Sense II, 27–34, 43, 44; as solution, 30, 31, 43, 179; successful use of, 30, 31; as synonym for response or reply, 30, 31, 43, 179
A priori effort, 75–85
Argument: in Sense I, 21, 44, 47–48, 60–61, 92, 180, 188; in Sense II, 21, 44, 47–48, 60–61, 92, 140, 180, 188; sound, 14, 15, 16; "substantial," 19; two senses of, 21, 109, 180; use of (Capricious, 37, 61, 80, 90, 92, 186, 188–89; cogent, 184, 185; demonstrable, 43–44, 59–60, 67–68; metaphysical, 6, 47, 48, 60, 67, 84–85, 89–90, 96, 119; moral, 6, 84–85, 89–90; persuasive, 43–44, 60, 67–68; Purist, 37, 80, 90, 92, 96, 186; rigorous, 14, 15); valid, 14, 15, 16, 19
Arguments: analytical, 13; educational, 4, 5, 6, 12, 13, 14, 15, 20, 36, 37, 90–91, 96, 97, 109–10, 119, 179, 180; empirical, 22; evaluative, 5, 15, 16, 20, 22, 36, 37, 38, 96, 139, 140, 172; formal, 14, 22; informal, 36; metaphysical, 6, 38, 89, 90, 119, 126; moral, 6, 38, 83–85, 140; *see also* Moral reasons
Aristotle, 20, 106, 155, 186
Asking, 32–33
Assent distinguished from consent, 174–75
Assertion, 121, 165
Ayer, Alfred J., 85, 88 n. 23

Bambrough, Renford, 24
Beliefs: educational, 61; metaphysical, 48–49, 53, 60, 66, 67, 83, 114, 127; moral, 127
"Believe-in" distinguished from "believe-that," 121, 132; *see also* Bliks
Berkson, Isaac B., 73, 74
Berlin, Isaiah, 24, 170
Bliks, 119–28, 135, 183; and assertion, 121; educational, 119–28; metaphysical, 119–20; theological, 119–20
Braithwaite, R., 135
Brameld, Theodore, 10, 32, 33, 86 n. 9
Broudy, Harry S., 9, 44–45, 48–51, 57, 60, 66
Burnett, Joe, 49–51, 62 n. 7

Canons of criticism, 4, 5, 6, 110–11, 117–19, 124, 128, 138, 179; Scheffler's two modes of, 117, 124
Claims, 17–18, 34, 165; and counter-claims, 64 n. 14
Cohen, Morris R., 173 n. 11
"Community persuasion," 72
Conant, James B., 10–11, 129 n. 12
Conception of a good education, 87 n. 22
Consensual effort, 72–75
Consensus as identified with morality, 150
Consent; *see* Assent as distinguished from consent
Cooley, John C., 19–20
Copi, Irving, 66 n. 38
Criticism; *see* Canons of criticism; Prophylactic criticism distinguished from therapeutic, 90
Counts, G., 32, 33

Defeasible clause, 153
Definitions: educational, 45–46, 61, 112; persuasive, 46, 47, 57–58, 63–65, 81, 83, 97, 176; programmatic, 47, 64 (Scheffler's conception of criticized, 64 n. 13)
Demonstration; *see* Argument: use of
Deniability condition, 160–63, 189; *see also* Falsification
Denial, 153, 157
Deontological or Intuitionist viewpoint, 75
Derivative approach; *see* Metaphysical approach in education
Desideratum, 71, 154, 155, 166
"Desirability characterization," 70–72
Dewey, John, 17, 20, 28, 47, 65 n. 24, 69, 117–18, 131 n. 24, 135

Educational arguments; *see* Arguments
Educational conclusion, 126–27, 129 n. 10
Educational definitions; *see* Definitions
Educational ends, goals, or purposes, 9–12, 68, 71, 131–32, 134, 137–38
Educational metaphors; *see* Metaphors
Educational policies, 66, 67, 68, 87–88, 110, 125, 134
Educational proposals, 65 n. 24, 113, 114, 131, 167; curricular, 68, 113
Educational purposes in relation to metaphors, 109, 112–16
Educational theory; *see* Theory

Emulation, 156, 166
Ends of education, 68, 71; expressed as goals, 134
Evaluative arguments in education, 5, 16; *see also* Arguments: evaluative
Evaluative meaning, 77
Exceptive clause, 151, 152; *see also* Deniability condition
Explication, 113

Falsification, 141, 145, 159, 160, 162–63, 166, 170, 183; *see also* Deniability condition
"Family resemblance," 120
Flew, Anthony, 52, 121, 163
Foster, M. B., 174 n. 16
Frankena, William K., 83, 96–111, 125–26, 136, 137, 182

Gellner, Ernest A., 147–48
"Good enough" reason, 143–48, 159, 160–63, 167–72, 183, 188–89
"Good" reason, 140, 141, 143–48, 149, 151, 153, 159, 162, 165, 167–72
Gowin, D. Bob, 62 n. 7
"Great Debate" in education, 9–12

Hare, Richard M., 4, 68, 77, 82, 89, 92, 119–21, 141–42, 145–48
Hart, H. L. A., 18, 153
Heidegger, Martin, 60
Hook, Sidney, 9, 13, 49–50, 55–57, 65 n. 20, 67, 95
Horne, H., 60, 61 n. 1
Horsburgh, J., 132 n. 37
Hospers, John, 150
Hume, David, 22, 34, 55, 57, 74, 102, 106, 120, 123, 125, 180, 183
Hutchins, Robert, 10, 12, 28, 47, 114, 116, 135

Ideological principle distinguished from moral principle, 149
Implication, 51–52, 55–56, 58, 59, 65, 68, 100, 113–14; causal, 57; definitional, 57; educational, 50–51, 57, 60, 65–66 (in Sense I, 60; in Sense II, 59); formal, 57; logical, 49, 100, 113, 129; material, 57; metaphysical, 64; persuasive, 52, 57, 58–59; programmatic, 57, 58
Indoctrination, 164, 165, 167, 176 n. 26; and Scheffler's definition of teaching, 176 n. 26
Instrumental effort, 69, 176 n. 25
Instrumental Principle, 158–63, 166

James, William, 95
"Justifiable" premise, 103–4, 107–8, 110
Justification, 44, 55, 58–59, 79, 84, 100, 110, 144; *see also* "Good enough" reason

Kant, Immanuel, 38, 133, 146, 154, 176 n. 25
Kaplan, Abraham, 33, 35, 181
Kilpatrick, W., 117
Komisar, P., 64

Logic: formal, 14; as "generalized jurisprudence," 17; *see also* Argument

McClellan, James E., 62–64, 79, 84, 185

McGucken, William J., 26–28, 33, 34, 35, 38, 188
McMurray, Foster, 62 n. 7
McMurrin, Sterling, 95, 97–98
Maritain, J., 64 n. 12
Mayer, Martin, 11
Metaphor: Dewey's, of the school as embryo of society, 118; Plato's, of the cave, 118; otherworldly, 118; *see also* Metaphors; Bliks
Metaphors, 109–19, 126–28, 130–31; educational, 109–10, 112, 115, 117, 126, 131; epistemologically-oriented, 118; metaphysical, 114–15, 118; "root metaphors," 112–15, 118, 221; social, 112, 114; theological, 118; *see also* Bliks
Metaphysical approach in education, 49, 125; constructive, 49, 53, 60, 89; derivative, 49, 52, 60, 89
Metaphysical arguments, 59–60, 67, 96, 112, 119; canons of criticism applied to, 112; in education, 59–60, 67, 119; intentional and success uses of distinguished, 84–85; in Senses I and II, 61; *see also* Argument
Metaphysical beliefs; *see* Beliefs
Metaphysical premise, 98–99, 109–12, 119, 124–27, 129
Metaphysics, 48–49, 56, 67, 105–7; *see also* Metaphysical approach in education
Mill, John Stuart, 20
Moore, George E., 38, 47, 68, 79, 101, 104
Moral acts, 151
Moral arguments, 72, 83–85, 134; in education, 69
Moral education, 155
Moral language, 168
Moral premises, 127
Moral principle, 145, 148–49; *see also* Ideological principle
Moral reasons, 171
Morris, Van Cleve, 33

Nagel, Ernest, 173 n. 11
Nielsen, Kai, 132 n. 37
Nowell-Smith, 43

O'Connor, Daniel J., 53, 132 n. 37
"Open question" argument, 79, 87–88, 101, 150
Overriding reason, 151, 153, 188

Paley, William, 122, 123, 127, 183
Pepper, Stephen C., 118
Pedagogical principle, 163–67; *see also* Rule of relevance
Perkinson, H., 62 n. 7
Persuasive definition; *see* Definitions
Phenix, Philip, 175 n. 19
Philosophical arguments in education, 109; *see also* Arguments
Picture-preference, 113–14
Plato, 106, 118, 128, 134, 154, 189
Policy statement, Board of Education, New York City, 122–23, 125
Popper, Karl, 176 n. 24, 189
Principle of Defeasible Partiality, 73
Proof, 184, 189, 190
Prophylactic criticism distinguished from therapeutic, 90
Purist-Capricious impasse, 37, 90–92, 109, 128, 138, 172, 182, 184, 185

Question: answered by metaphysical argument, 60–61; answered in Senses I and II, 27; intended in Senses I and II, 27; meaningless, 60–61; metaphysical, 60; philosophical, dilemma of, 31; "should" type, 63, 72
Questions: answers to factual, formal, metaphysical, philosophical, 33; deliberative, 24, 25, 63; difficulties in answering, 39; in education, 32; evaluative, 24, 25, 32, 35, 140; factual, 24–25, 54; formal, 24, 25; inquisitive, 24; mathematical, 25; metaphysical, 24, 44; philosophical, 24, 33, 34; scientific, 25

Raup, R. Bruce, 72, 73, 86 n. 9
Rebuttal notion, 179, 187–89; *see also* Deniability condition
Reductio ad absurdam, 44, 59, 92
Religion: clarifying concept of, 45; teaching of, 62
"Root metaphor," 112–16, 119; *see also* Metaphors; Bliks
Rule of relevance, 163–67; *see also* Pedagogical principle
Ryle, Gilbert, 31, 44, 92, 134, 138, 157

Scheffler, Israel, 12, 31, 62 n. 4, 91, 110–12, 117, 118, 122, 124–27, 130 n. 21, 136, 176 n. 26, 182
Sheed, F. J., 75
"Should" questions; *see* Questions
Sleeper, Ralph W., 86 n. 7, 132 n. 37
Smart, J. C. C., 136–37
Smith, B. Othanel, 64 n. 14, 105, 106, 108, 110, 111, 114, 116, 118, 131 nn. 24 and 30, 136, 183
Smullyan, Arthur, 14, 16, 17, 19, 20, 23, 36, 103, 142, 180, 184
Social metaphor; *see* Metaphor
Solution; *see* Answer
Spencer, Herbert, 25–28, 32, 33, 34, 35, 37, 38, 44, 140, 180, 187–88
Spinoza, Benedict, 155
Stevenson, Charles, 46, 63 n. 9, 156
Supererogatory acts, 156
Synoptic and visionary function of philosophy, 135, 191

Task words, 31
Teaching, 163–172; of atheism, 161; of attitudes, 138–40; definition of, 176 n. 25; of doubting, 176 n. 25; of evolution, 145; of falsehood, 149, 152–53, 157, 162; of knowledge, 138–40; "meaningfully," 164, 165, 166 (method for, 167); of moral attitudes, 165–66; of patriotism, 141, 148; performative aspects of, 174 n. 15; persuasive definition of, 176 n. 26; related usages of, 176 n. 26; skills, 138–40; and "teaching-for," "-how," and "-that," 138–40; three conditions of, 164, 176; of true accounts, 158–63; of truth, 152–53
Test distinguished from testimony, 74–75
Theory: educational, 62–63, 99, 130; scientific, 63
Thomas, L. G., 70, 86 n. 8
Toulmin, Stephen, 16–20, 23, 43, 77, 90, 92, 180

Uncharacteristic virtues, 165
Universal premises, 146, 148–49

Universalizable principle, 146–58, 183; distinguished from E-type valuation, 146–48, 152–56; and U-type valuation, 146-58
Use of argument; *see* Argument

Value judgment, 15
Verification principle, 35

Waismann, Frederick, 62 n. 6, 92
"Warranted assertibility," 72
Watkins, J. W. N., 6, 157, 190
"We" in education, 174 n. 16
Wittgenstein, Ludwig, 60
Woodring, Paul, 9, 176 n. 25